The Secularization of Sin

The
Secularization
of Sin

An Investigation
of the Daedalus Complex

Richard K. Fenn

Westminster/John Knox Press
Louisville, Kentucky

Book design by Ken Taylor

First edition

Published by Westminster/John Knox Press
Louisville, Kentucky

PRINTED IN THE UNITED STATES OF AMERICA
9 8 7 6 5 4 3 2 1

Library of Congress Cataloging-in-Publication Data

Fenn, Richard K.
    The secularization of sin / Richard K. Fenn. — 1st ed.
        p.   cm.
    Includes bibliographical references and index.
    ISBN 0-664-25189-7

    1. Sociology, Christian—United States.   2. Guilt—Religious aspects—Christianity.   3. Guilt and culture—United States.
4. Secularism—United States.   5. Pastoral psychology.   6. United States—Social conditions—1980–   7. United States—Church history—20th century.   I. Title.
BR517.F45   1991
261—dc20   91-3323

To John Ordway

Daedalus

When he fell
did blue heaven
empty,
momentarily
an abyss
above the dark
sky he stunned?

—Kimball Fenn

Contents

Acknowledgments

In a book on debt, it is more than appropriate for me to acknowledge a wide variety of debts that I have to those whose friendship and professional help have encouraged me to write this book. Of all such debts, the most personal is to John Ordway, a professional himself in the understanding of unconscious obligations.

There are three members of the professional staff at Princeton Theological Seminary without whom this book would not ever have reached the point of publication. They are Joe Herman, Denise Schwalb, and Jerry Gorham: a trio of excellent secretaries and professional assistants.

There are other debts, most of which are too elusive to be specified and belong to the context in which this book was written. Princeton Theological Seminary establishes a climate in which explorations of this sort are supported and called for. My close colleague at the seminary, Don Capps, has given me many hours of collegial support and stimulation.

I should mention also Jim and Leila Day in Castine, Maine, whose generosity provided me space over a long sabbatical for the writing of the first draft of this manuscript. Castine is another such context that is conducive to long hours of thinking and writing surrounded by friends.

I wish finally to acknowledge the inspiration I have received from Caroline, my wife; from our daughters, Caroline and Kimball; and from our son, Tom: all dear beyond words.

RICHARD K. FENN

Castine, Maine

Introduction:

How Religion Perpetuates the Vicious Circle of Desire, Devotion, Dread, and Sacrifice

If it is dangerous for modern societies to allow their educational, religious, and political rites to fall into disrepute or disrepair, it is a disaster for traditional societies that lack other means of recruiting, mobilizing, and controlling their members. That is one of the warnings implicit in the myth of Daedalus and Icarus.

Daedalus

The labyrinth from which Theseus escaped by means of the clew of Ariadne was built by Daedalus, a most skilful artificer. It was an edifice with numberless winding passages and turnings opening into one another, and seeming to have neither beginning nor end, like the river Maeander, which returns on itself, and flows now onward, now backward, in its course to the sea. Daedalus built the labyrinth for King Minos, but afterwards lost the favour of the king, and was shut up in a tower. He contrived to make his escape from prison, but could not leave the island by sea, as the king kept strict watch on all the vessels, and permitted none to sail without being carefully searched. "Minos may control the land and sea," said Daedalus, "but not the regions of the air. I will try that way." So he set to work to fabricate wings for himself and his young son Icarus. He wrought feathers together, beginning with the smallest and adding larger, so as to form an increasing surface. The larger ones he secured with thread and the smaller with wax, and gave the whole a gentle curvature like the wings of a bird. Icarus, the boy, stood and looked on, sometimes

running to gather up the feathers which the wind had
blown away, and then handling the wax and working it
over with his fingers, by his play impeding his father in his
labours. When at last the work was done, the artist, waving
his wings, found himself buoyed upward, and hung sus-
pended, poising himself on the beaten air. He next
equipped his son in the same manner and taught him how
to fly, as a bird tempts her young ones from the lofty nest
into the air. When all was prepared for flight he said, "Icarus, my son, I charge you to keep at a moderate height, for
if you fly too low the damp will clog your wings, and if too
high the heat will melt them. Keep near me and you will be
safe." While he gave him these instructions and fitted the
wings to his shoulders, the face of the father was wet with
tears, and his hands trembled. He kissed the boy, not knowing that it was for the last time. Then rising on his wings, he
flew off, encouraging him to follow, and looked back from
his own flight to see how his son managed his wings. As
they flew the ploughman stopped his work to gaze, and the
shepherd leaned on his staff and watched them, astonished
at the sight, and thinking they were gods who could thus
cleave the air.

They passed Samos and Delos on the left and Lebynthos
on the right, when the boy, exulting in his career, began to
leave the guidance of his companion and soar upward as if
to reach heaven. The nearness of the blazing sun softened
the wax which held the feathers together, and they came
off. He fluttered with his arms, but no feathers remained to
hold the air. While his mouth uttered cries to his father it
was submerged in the blue waters of the sea, which thence-
forth was called by his name. His father cried, "Icarus, Icarus, where are you?" At last he saw the feathers floating on
the water, and bitterly lamenting his own arts, he buried
the body and called the land Icaria in memory of his child.
Daedalus arrived safe in Sicily, where he built a temple to
Apollo, and hung up his wings, an offering to the god.

Daedalus was so proud of his achievements that he could
not bear the idea of a rival. His sister had placed her son
Perdix under his charge to be taught the mechanical arts.

He was an apt scholar and gave striking evidences of ingenuity. Walking on the seashore he picked up the spine of a fish. Imitating it, he took a piece of iron and notched it on the edge, and thus invented the saw. He put two pieces of iron together, connecting them at one end with a rivet, and sharpening the other ends, and made a pair of *compasses*. Daedalus was so envious of his nephew's performances that he took an opportunity, when they were together one day on the top of a high tower, to push him off. But Minerva, who favors ingenuity, saw him falling, and arrested his fate by changing him into a bird called after his name, the Partridge. This bird does not build his nest in the trees, nor take lofty flights, but nestles in the hedges, and mindful of his fall, avoids high places. (Bulfinch, pp. 128–129)

Daedalus's work is obscure. If it was an initiation rite of some sort, it was the work of Daedalus both as father and as craftsman. Indeed, the term "craftsman" also applies to the priests of various mystery cults, who were licensed to introduce their followers to the mysteries. In these cults various desires were stimulated; some were satisfied, and any residues of unsatisfied desires were transformed into new obligations. Thus young women became matrons. Young men became adult males. The terrors of death were imitated and fear assuaged. Human beings' "fundamental flaw" was healed in rites that promised to deliver purification from the ills of despair, illness, and mortality.

Of course, these newly created obligations were not readily linked with those of the *polis,* which sought to attract these investments of energy and desire by making its own heroes the center of devotion. Furthermore, all rites, mysterious or civic, often fail. That is the point; ritual is a brittle method for transforming desire into duty. When there is only one set of rites on which a society depends, therefore, those rites must be carefully guarded; the temple must be preserved. When the rites fail or the temple is destroyed, the community scatters or is destroyed. Conviction of an original sin becomes prevalent.

The Daedalus Myth

It may well be, in fact, that the Daedalus myth is a clue to some traditional mystery cult and its rites. Many of the elements of purification by cultic initiation are there. One is purified by water and by fire, by being submerged or washed and also by being singed and scourged (cf. Burkert 1985:76). Certainly Icarus suffered the fate of those who, unprepared for the mysteries, receive its encounters with water and fire as punishments rather than as the gateways to purification. There are also hints of mystery initiations in the myth's mention of the labyrinth. In his analysis of the experience of initiates, Burkert (1987:91ff.) notes that they no doubt became confused by being forced to wander in strange paths; certainly a labyrinth would provide ample confusion, so that one would not know how to return to the beginning or find one's way out at the end, and it may well be that certain cults employed a labyrinth as part of their initiation. In such mazes, furthermore, may have been the representations of monsters: lions breathing fire or other beasts that, like a Minotaur, might well have frightened initiates and produced, as Burkert (1987:91ff.) reminds us, genuine anxiety or even terror. Those who made their way through safely enjoyed a vision, not unlike the elevated vista that may have greeted Daedalus and Icarus on their flight, along with a sight of the impure and unenlightened masses below.

There may also be reminiscences here of the purification of citizens returning from a foreign land or of soldiers returning from war, since Athens had not forgotten its battles with King Minos; Apollo, to whom Bulfinch has Daedalus sacrificing at the end, purified the believer from bloodguilt (Burkert 1985:77). The possibilities are complex, but the point is simple: Rites of purification may well underlie the Daedalus myth.

More likely, perhaps, than a mystery rite is the possibility that scapegoating of some kind underlies the Daedalus myth. Burkert (1985:82ff.) reports that the young, the poor, the criminal, the ugly, and the strange or the vulnerable were often singled out by a city seeking to rid itself of the evil in its midst, to expunge its fundamental fault. Apparently Pilate also was familiar with a rite in which a criminal was set free, only to be dressed in vestments, wreathed, scourged, and marched around the city to cries of hatred and derision, all prior to the killing of the victim himself. It is a way of purging a city of its troubles, and in this respect Jerusalem had many antecedents in antiquity. Burkert makes it clear that many victims were similarly honored with mock attentions before being humiliated and led to their deaths. In two cities victims were plunged into the sea:

> From the cliffs of Leukas in the precinct of Apollo, Leukas, a condemned criminal, was plunged into the sea every year; he was, however, provided with wings to lighten his leap and an attempt was made to fish him up again. Another report speaks of a young man being plunged into the sea for Poseidon, in order to be rid of all evil with him: "become our offscourings" (*peripsema*). (Burkert 1985:83)

Now, the priests of various cults were precisely those required to get rid of the offscourings of various sacrifices—to dispose of the remains of the animals (or perhaps humans) sacrificed. The priest as Daedalus may therefore have had two tasks: to dispose of the offscourings of mystery rites and to dispose of human offscourings into the sea from some high place. Adolescents were occasionally sacrificed to Athena to atone for sacrilege, and the theme of such sacrifice may also appear in initiation rites (Burkert 1985:84). It is clear that the

Daedalus myth may tap rites of communal purification (e.g., the criminal outfitted with wings) as well as rites in which the priest urged the initiate to follow him carefully lest he plunge to death in the sea or be horrifyingly scourged by fire. Perhaps memories of murdering victims for the sake of purifying a city lie close to the surface of the myth, barely submerged beneath whatever embellishment the myth contains in symbol and allegory. The dread of Daedalus—that something terrible might happen—would therefore be rooted in memories of actual sacrifice.

Once again we find ourselves confronted with the connection between initiation into life and initiation into death. In the funeral rites of rural Greece the women still sing laments that compare death with a marriage or a wedding with a funeral. Many of the words and much of the music are interchangeable: a few set pieces to dramatize the transition from one state to another, from being at home to being away, from being safely enclosed among friends and family to being among strangers. The way is perilous, the passage dark. Departures such as these are terribly disturbing for the ones leaving and for the ones left behind. Everyday life is a sea of tranquility compared with these rough passages. To navigate into the safe harbor or to disembark at the farther shore requires a pilot and a guide—one who can say, with Daedalus, "Follow me." Avoid the heights and the depths. Mark your way carefully to the homeland, where you shall rest from your labors, where your strivings shall cease. Remember Freud's pleasure principle: the wish for the Nirvana of the beginning and the end. Both are quiet; it is the passage that is tumultuous and full of danger.

The goal of these rites of purification is to restore the original harmonies of life in the present and even after death. As I will argue in chapter 6, there is no room within the maternal matrix for a fundamental, fatal flaw.

The end is like the beginning: a place of wholeness. Of course the shrines and sanctuaries of antiquity combine features of the grave, therefore, and of the womb. Caves, grottoes, springs, hollows in the rock, pools of water—the natural sites of birth and of death form the setting of the sacred (Burkert 1985:84–87). Even in Athens the Acropolis enjoys a small, salty pool within the Erechtheion itself; open to the sky yet surrounded by the north hall, it is an inner space where heaven is reflected on earth (Burkert 1985:86), the maternal body, where only the purified can enter. One approaches it with longing and with fear and trembling—that is, with a sense of sin.

Outside the temple, one can offer sacrifices and engage in the imaginary purification or rescue of the body and soul; yet only the priests, the most pure of all, can enter the temple itself. They enter not only on their own behalf, of course, but on behalf of the people themselves. In this constellation of people and place, one sees reenacted the imaginary world of childhood. There the infant has the imaginary power of life and death; its thoughts, like the prayers of the adult devotee, seal the fate of the self and others. There the votive offerings, the early precursor of the modern vote, augur well-being for the society and the individual if the rites are properly followed. It is an uncanny world, as Freud pointed out, because the uncanny is the world of the infant, full of imaginary powers, where gestures and words are omnipotent and fateful.

Both the modern rites and the ancient ones require sacrifices of the purse and the intellect. In the ancient rites, however, the sense of the uncanny was considerably more palpable. Remember that even the priest-craftsman himself, the Daedalus, approached the rite of passage with dread, lest something terrible happen. Whether the sacrifices were real or imaginary, in blood or with libations, human or animal, the sense of dread suggests that the powers of life and death are at work. Where, then, is the comparable sense of dread in modern rites, whether of the voting booth or of the many initiations that mark the passage from childhood into adulthood?

In the sacrifices conducted before the temple, it is clear that one's life is lived at others' expense. "He died for us" is precisely the expression of the sacrificing mentality. It was clear, when the community pushed the criminal over the cliff, that the peace of the city had been restored at the price of human life. It is somewhat less clear in, for instance, the modern classroom, where each seat represents a considerable sacrifice. The places occupied by those in the classroom are not available to others who might aspire to the privilege; even in private schools the cost of education is hardly defrayed by tuition. Sacrifices of the intellect and of the purse are also required in the modern classroom, but the sacrifices are small, routine, daily, even banal. Although few flee from the scene as though something *terrible* has happened, absenteeism is nevertheless chronic. Indeed, it is the absence of drama that makes dread of the classroom a subject for the cartoon strip rather than for the priestly craft. The rites of "Greek" fraternities and sororities remain, but they are pale travesties of the original mysteries. Where, then, is a sense of dread at entering the world of the uncanny, where the imaginary powers of infancy are invoked to create and preserve life or to ward off death?

The rites of transition in any society may at times fail to inspire an appropriate sense of dread. The desire for access to the sources of life and fear of reprisal from rivals to that infantile success are not then transformed into religious devotion. The surplus of devotion, so to speak, is not replenished with a new supply from each generation of initiates and devotees. The reduction of duty to desire prevents the transformation of desire into duty. Sociologists then issue tracts against the rise of individualism or analyze the causes of cynicism and apathy among the young, in the electorate, or in others who do not value what passes for the franchise. In antiquity myths provided the cautionary comment that the youth, impeding their fathers' work, may not be prepared to undertake the long and perilous journey into adulthood.

The Dread of Separation

In this book I focus on dread of lasting separation from the maternal matrix; as the roots of these words imply, the original matrix is the mother. Now, the extent of longing for such a return may vary from one person to the next and from one time in life to another. Certainly entire peoples have gone through periods of intense longing for such a return to their original place in the world. It would be difficult to find any anxiety more pervasive than the fear that one will be unable to return from exile to one's homeland.

Such dread can be transformed into a sense of one's fate; those destined to remain abroad even until death share a different fate from those who can look forward to a return. That is precisely Anderson's (1983) thesis on the rise of nationalism in the Americas: Those Spaniards whose itineraries did *not* allow them to return to the peninsula at the end of their careers found themselves in the new world on quite a different footing and sharing quite a different fate from the one anticipated by imperial emissaries destined to return. I would expect a similar sense of national identity to have formed in antiquity in the peoples whose ancestry could be traced to the Greek peninsula; those who could return must have seemed—like Icarus and Daedalus—"like gods" to those who were fated to remain on land far from their spiritual home.

The desire to return to one's original matrix does not bring out the best in one's character but rather envy, resentment, hatred, and a desire to turn the tables on those who are occupying one's rightful place. Consider Israel in antiquity. Neusner (1987:60) argues that the experience of such resentment became a way of life sanctioned and reproduced by the Torah from one generation to the next, making it impossible to forget the exile of one's people even long after the return. It was that resentment, of course, that fueled hostility not only toward the non-Jewish people who also occupied the land but toward the Jews who had not left Israel. While it is the one returning from foreign lands who is in need of purification, the returning Jews managed to turn the tables by arguing that it was the residents, the "poor" of the land, who were insufficiently purified; hence the beginning of a Judaism that, in its Pharisaic development, continued to make resentment into a motive for domination of the laity and for making them take on the role of priests in everyday life (cf. Neusner 1987:59).

Daedalus, too, on his return, found that a nephew had been making a name for himself as an innovator and craftsman; in effect, he had taken Daedalus's place. The myth indicates that Daedalus sought to eliminate Perdix entirely. The nephew was saved only by Wisdom, Minerva, and was only allowed to maintain a low and undistinguished profile. Wisdom may well be the virtue of those who are not entitled to claim a central place in the cult or an ancient right to the land itself.

Stripped of its poignancy and note of longing, however, the desire for return to the land, to one's source in the original matrix, is a particularly consuming and potentially destructive passion. That is why I am treating it here as the basis of sin: the fatal fault underlying both anger and envy. Although such a statement may seem unsympathetic to the struggles of expatriots and exiles to recover their homelands, it is realistic in view of the destructive consequences of an ideology of triumphant return. Just such an ideology was developed by the returning Jewish exiles after the destruction of the first Temple; that is Neusner's (1987) point about the ideology of Judaism as it developed after the return and during the temporarily successful Maccabean revolt. Purity would be the consummate virtue of a people disciplined in every aspect of their lives and so entitled to dispossess, if need be, those who also claimed an ancestral right and an uninterrupted occupation of the land.

The underlying motives of anger and envy also inform some of the mythology of the period of the return, which depicts the non-Jewish people, the enemies of Israel, as devouring beasts. Mendels (1987:19ff.) describes in some detail the bestial imagery of the writer of 1 Enoch, who is witnessing the beginnings of a period that, he hopes, will restore Israel's sovereignty and Temple cult in the land. I do not mean for one minute to minimize the tragedy of the losses sustained by Israel at the hands of the Babylonians, Seleucids, and Ptolemies, and eventually of the Romans as well. The point is that the dread of annihilation fosters the most destructive and passionate demands for sole possession of one's place of origin, whether that is an ancestral land or the womb itself. Psychoanalysis roots the dread of neighbors, rivals, and enemies in this all-consuming and most exclusive passion for sole access to the source of life. As the danger one feels without such access is the threat of annihilation, so the punishment of one's rivals must take the form of annihilation. The devouring beasts who threaten Israel must be destroyed. That is why the "enemy as beast" is a symbol of this most primitive and diffuse passion not only for survival but also for command over the sources of one's organic and spiritual life.

Dread at the loss of the land, of one's place in the world, is clearly too human and universal to be monopolized by any one people, but it was Israel that made such dread a way of life. In what Neusner (1987:41) calls the "exegesis of the everyday as a sequence of acts of sancti-

fication," Israel after the exile institutionalized the
dread of losing one's home, one's land, one's very life.
Thanks to the priests, that dread focused on the ability to
make pilgrimage to the Temple, to support its sacrifices,
and to uphold the Torah. However, the priests made the
Torah, as a set of instructions on everyday living, the
means of forestalling the dreaded loss of the nurturing
and supporting matrix of the homeland. That was why
the fear of pollution became chronic and the demand for
purification intense. As I have argued, it is the presence
of unwanted others in the maternal matrix, within the
womb or in infancy, that instills the fear of pollution, of
being invaded in one's own most intimate space by foreign matter. It is the competition with such rivals, I have
argued, that underlies the demand for purification.
Neusner incidentally confirms the argument when he
notes:

> The purpose [of priestly Judaism] was to define Israel
> against the background of the other peoples of the Near
> and Middle East, with whom Israel had much in common, and
> especially to differentiate Israel from its near relations and
> neighbors—for example, Samaritans—in the same country.
> (1987:41)

It might seem that the only dread here is existential:
the definition of the self alongside others who are not
quite entitled to a share in the matrix of one's origin.
Why then would dread of this sort, not as intense as the
dread of losing one's initial place, require such strenuous methods of purification? The others with rights to
occupy that primal space included even those Jews who
had never gone into exile; they had enjoyed uninterrupted residence within the homeland. Instead of making these people the "older brother," so to speak,
against whom the prodigal younger brother seeks to establish a right to return, the priestly reforms defined
them, the "people of the land," as being impure.

Neusner (1987:37–38) states that the priestly reforms under Ezra required that the returning Jews divorce the wives they had married from among these people; they were to be put outside the system in order for the system to be purified of all those with a rival claim to the original space.

It may seem harsh to suggest that Israel turned dread into a way of life. It is tantamount to saying that, thanks to the priestly code, the people adopted a neurosis as standard for the nation. Now, a neurosis is an unsolved conflict, only the symptoms of which may be visible, for example, in rites of self-purification or in masochistic forms of self-denial and renunciation, as in the divorcing of wives who would otherwise be loved and acceptable. Nonetheless, as I read him, this outstanding scholar of Israel's history is making precisely this point. Neusner, speaking of the Torah, argues that "religion did more than merely recapitulate resentment; it precipitated it by selecting as events only a narrow sample of what had happened, and by imparting to that selection of events meanings pertinent to only a few" (1987:34).

That is precisely what characterizes certain neuroses: a selective vision of the past that leaves out important details that might contradict the vision of tragic and undeserved suffering; it is a vision carefully interpreted in ways that only those who understand and share the vision can appreciate. Amply elaborated, with the details carefully woven together according to the underlying logic, the neurosis can dominate all aspects of everyday life as well as the moments in which it is more dramatically exhibited.

What then underlies the neurosis? What is the conflict left unconscious and unresolved? The conflict is between the longing to return and the humiliation that must precede any eventual triumph. Remember, for instance, Reik's insistence that masochism is wedded to suffering precisely because it is the punishment that must accompany any triumph that eliminates rivals and initiates glorious satisfaction; hence the dread that one will be unable to enjoy undisturbed and untroubled the promised land of one's origin. As Neusner puts it, the demand created by the myth "created expectations that could not be met" (1987:34). I take him to mean that all obsessive forms of purification will never fully relieve the dread of loss of one's matrix; purification never works once and for all and must therefore be continuously repeated with increasingly severe rites of renunciation. The demand for purification in fact "renewed the resentment captured by the myth of exile" (Neusner 1987:34) and so intensified longings for triumphal return. It is a vicious cycle indeed.

It is possible, then, that conflicting fears and desires can interact, form a system, intensify one another, and come to dominate not only the spectacle of the theater or collective rites of purification but also the routines of everyday life. Dreams of national glory can require a preliminary period of suffering and a penultimate struggle with the nation's enemies: a disaster, in fact, before the dawn of victory. On the other hand, rites of purification, painful sacrifices, and careful attention to purity in everyday life can promise, if followed carefully, to prevent just such a disaster by making a nation safe against its rivals. It is possible that the Daedalus myth reflects a religious system that sought to forestall the very disaster that it predicted and required as a prelude to triumph. The myth may also have been associated with a ritual that had to be repeated periodically to ensure that disaster would be anticipated and postponed.

Religious systems are therefore self-perpetuating; they may even be self-fulfilling, as Neusner (1987) chooses to describe the long-term effects of Israel's myth and ritual. Certainly, the myth provides a principle for self-selection and the selection or rejection of others; it roots these choices, that otherwise might lack legitimacy, in a divine election of the chosen nation (cf. Luhmann 1984). The system works as long as the priests or intellectuals who promote the ideology can find subscribers in other elements of the population.

In bad times, in fact, the subscribers grow in number for a variety of reasons that are only dimly grasped by such terms as "cognitive dissonance." Communities and ethnic groups in modern Europe and North America tend to embrace their symbols of communal identity more firmly as the communities themselves become threatened by outside forces and the erosion of their boundaries by people, money, ideas, and other foreign elements. There was a similar disparity between the social facts and the Israelite myth; Neusner reminds us that

> the stress on exclusion of the neighbors from the group, and of the group from the neighbors, ran contrary to the situation of ancient Israel, with the unmarked frontiers of culture and the constant giving and receiving among diverse groups which were generally characteristic of ancient times. (1987:32)

From Desire to Devotion

In this book I am concerned with the need for purification in order to avoid what Reik (1957; 1970:18ff.) at various points calls the dread of punishment, the dread of loss of love, or the "dreaded authority." There are many personal forms of purification in modern societies; I would not be surprised to find that much of the current emphasis on meditation, exercise, and diet is a way of alleviating feelings of guilt for which there is little in the way of public knowledge, language, or recognition. In societies based primarily on kinship ties, as Reik writes (1957; 1970:34–38), there was also a sense of guilt that required purification for its relief, but this sense was communal as well as personal:

The books of Westermarck, Durkheim, Robertson Smith and
other scholars present an abundance of instances from ancient history and primitive tribes which prove that solidarity of the family or of the clan implies also responsibility
for the crime of the individual. (1957; 1970:36)

In modern societies, he argues, the collective sense of
guilt is not well articulated; the public discourse of
journalists and politicians provides little evidence that
such collective guilt actually exists. Nonetheless, Reik
insists that the widespread popular sense of guilt and
depression after the dropping of the atomic bombs on
Hiroshima and Nagasaki was strong enough to lead to
self-defeating consequences or even a subtle form of
mass masochism. That is precisely my point as well: that
the sense of guilt in modern societies can indeed take on
such subtle and negative consequences because we lack
the theater and the rites by which whole societies might
purify themselves of the crimes of individuals.

Take, for example, the problem of soldiers who return
from war. In many tribes, Reik argues, returning soldiers
were subjected to "atoning and purifying rituals" (1957;
1970:37) so that their societies would not be haunted by
the avenging souls of the enemy that had been slain. Such
rituals are conspicuously absent in the United States, despite the public expressions, for instance, of guilt and
remorse for the war in Vietnam, in which many noncom-
batants as well as foreign soldiers were killed, not to mention our own losses. It is clear that the Vietnam veterans
themselves bear an extraordinary burden of guilt as well as
resentment at having been treated as unclean and impure
by their fellow citizens on their return, as if the citizens
could relieve their guilt by ostracizing the veterans. The
lack of rites makes such guilt pervasive, intractable, and
perennially burdensome to the society as a whole.

The pathway from desire to devotion, then, begins
with the symbol of desire; here I have been emphasizing
the desire for return to the source of life, the womb

itself. It is a regressive wish, never stronger than when the individual faces a terribly uncertain future, such as on leaving home for a new family, for new duties, or for the dangers of a foreign land and of death itself.

The transition to a life of obligation is architecturally planned out in the passage from font to altar. In Greek sanctuaries there were often altars placed near the pit or the pool (Burkert 1985:87ff.). The devotion of the initiates to the god could be celebrated there; promises were made, gifts given, animals sacrificed, and vows taken. These devotions signified a reservoir of a different sort— not a pool of satisfied desire but a deep well from which societies could draw for the performance of duty. Promises were to be kept; gifts to the gods came with thanks and the vow to give again, should more wishes be granted. There was a certain exchange rate in the temple between the satisfaction of desire and the performance of duty. It was the function of the temple of antiquity to establish that exchange rate for the society at large.

Successful temples, of course, produced a large surplus of devotion, exceeding the cost of satisfying the desire of the worshipers. Indeed, many temples became repositories of gold and metal—treasuries of material as well as spiritual gifts. Tyrants were known to seize these treasures for financing their armies (Burkert 1985:94). The polis may also have drawn, in a more orderly fashion, on this surplus of devotion in order to finance its demands on the citizenry for attending to the work of the polis and the people, for paying tribute and taxes, and for maintaining public order.

It is the secret of society to turn desire into devotion and devotion into civic obligation. In antiquity it required priests and liturgies to turn the desire for nourishment and untroubled repose into a sense of obligation to maintain public order and welfare. Even the central shrines in the cities of antiquity, however, had competition from shrines in high places or distant

valleys. The center has always to look out for the shrines
on the periphery, where desire may turn into dissent
rather than duty. On the periphery of modern societies,
moreover, are cults that promise a peace of mind that
has no redeeming social value. Some religious movements still feature the satisfaction of regressive desires
for nourishment, repose, and eternal life without the
payment of tribute to the state or of tithes to the temple.
Such developments are obscene in the eyes of those
whose duty it is to tap private devotions for public purposes, lest the modern polis lose its major source of rev-
enue and moral commitment.

In the complex pathways offered to initiates as they
enter modern societies, the route from the satisfaction of
immediate desire to the performance of public duty is
devious, subtle, and full of more uncertainties than a
cultic labyrinth. Spiritual and psychological guides
promise techniques to satisfy personal longings within
legitimate social roles. "Studies" are continually "show-
ing" one how to relieve depression, enhance personal
growth, and make more headway in one's work or education. I am arguing that modern pathways are now
more devious, the guides and practitioners more jealous
of their crafts, and the eventual benefits to both the individual and society far more uncertain and costly than
was the case when slaughtering a pig or erecting a small
statue on the altar nearest the sacred pool was sufficient.

In the epilogue I write what C. Wright Mills once
called a "secular letter to the Christian clergy." It is a
secular letter because I am writing from the vantage
point of a sociologist who wants to ask the clergy some
questions. It is only fair to say, however, that as a minis-
ter myself I am writing to those whose dilemmas I have
experienced firsthand. We share the same commitment
to the world through the church.

One of my questions will concern the primitive debt
that I will have been describing throughout this book:

the often unnamed debt to the insatiable hunger that is sometimes called narcissism, at other times greed or merely "consuming passions." The Episcopal prayer book used to speak of "sinful desires and inordinate affections," but even that strong language does not quite go to the heart of the matter. This "debt to Eros" that causes a profound restlessness can also lead an individual to feel that he or she has missed the boat or failed to discharge some primordial debt. That feeling can make the clergy and the laity alike not only dissatisfied with their lives but also terribly vulnerable to demands from the church (let alone from the world) that they make one more sacrifice or give a little more. The debt to one's own greed gets projected onto the world. It is then the world's needs that remain unsatisfied, and indeed the world's hunger is profound.

What I am asking is whether the clergy tend to exploit the laity's sense of having an unpaid debt. There are dozens of ways it can be exploited, whether by appeals for tithing or appeals for relief work. Each appeal has its own merits, and I am not against either paying the church's bills (when they are moderate) or feeding the hungry. What concerns me is that these bills can never be paid in full simply because the debt to greed, to one's own greed, is never satisfied. Yes, it is some accomplishment to transform desire into obligation, so that the individual's unsatisfied hungers become shaped into an obligation to pay one's debt to the church, to various social institutions, and to the world. It is not enough, however, to help the laity make this transformation of desire into a sense of indebtedness.

Why not? It is not enough because it sets up both the clergy and the laity to pay more than the minimally necessary debt to society and its institutions, including the church. To begin with, the laity are led down labyrinthine paths—the complex paths of modern societies, like the labyrinth that Daedalus created for King Minos. At the heart of that labyrinth was the Minotaur, the greediest of all monsters, who sacrificed youth to the desire of the king. The whole myth is about that sacrificial complex, whether the complex is called civilization or simply social life. The laity are set up to give their time, talents, and energy in an endless life of service to the church and the world. The clergy know precisely how greedy and destructive the church itself can be; the church will easily consume not only their own lives but also their marriages and families, even their friendships and leisure time. It is understandable if they would like the laity to suffer with them in a life of perfect service. This is the church that Garrison Keillor called "Our Lady of Perpetual Responsibility." It can be a joyless communion.

Certainly it is not the clergy's fault that individuals are all too willing to serve greedy institutions or even just a greedy social system. The myth of the Minotaur and the labyrinth antedates the Christian community by several centuries. But the churches tell the story of a man who made extraordinary claims both for himself and his kingdom: a man who met a terrible death on the cross. A Greek of the first century might have seen in the fate of Icarus a parallel to the son (Jesus) who did not stay the middle course and was carried away, as it were, in his own dangerous trajectory too close to the gods. The point is that dreams of glory, when we entertain them and take them to heart, always exact a terrible psychic price; they require that we suffer first before we enter into glory. That is the origin of the masochistic character, and I am making that point here because I want to argue that religion—and the Protestant churches in particular—has been responsible for perpetuating the sacrificial system that I call in this book the Daedalus complex. To that extent the churches, and particularly the clergy, are still responsible for what has been a vicious circle of emotional debt, civic obligation, and the inevitable sacrifice of desire to obligation.

1

The Daedalus Complex

---→✶←---

It might seem strange that a religious culture like Christianity promises so much triumph but requires a lifetime of self-sacrifice. To put it another way: Why does a religion that promises freedom require its adherents to surrender their will to God? The promise, of course, is that such service brings "perfect freedom." It is like the promise that a lifetime of self-sacrifice will bring certain triumph over suffering and death—a triumph, not incidentally, over all one's obstacles, rivals, and enemies. In both cases, the promise recedes into the future and is known in the present only by anticipation; that is, by faith.

Reik (1957), as I have noted, finds the root cause of a lifetime of self-sacrifice, of a willingness to suffer indefinitely with no discernible reward except in the future, in masochism. In masochism the distant reward and its pleasures disappear from view. They reappear only in the apparent pleasure that the sufferer takes in his or her misfortune, illness, rejection, and failure. Reik puts it this way:

> The masochistic character enjoys the idea that he will finally carry through his will despite everything . . . [because] the aggressive and ambitious, revengeful and violent instinctual aims, the parrying of which resulted in the genesis of masochism, rise again in the expected and phantasied satisfaction [of eventual triumph]. (1957:319)

The underlying source of pleasure, then, is the source also of guilt; a fantasied triumph of the will over all who

stand in the masochist's way. The imagined triumph offers a certain pleasure in the midst of trials and sufferings. Those trials and sufferings, moreover, are the
punishment for imagining an eventual triumph over all
one's rivals and enemies. The unconscious law of an eye
for an eye, as Freud reminded us, requires that one suffer
the injuries one wishes to inflict on others. The unconscious, taking the wish for the deed, requires a lifetime
of self-punishment to atone for everlasting victory, even
a fantasied victory. At the heart of masochism, then, lies
greed: a destructive, all-consuming passion that, in the
end, leaves the greedy one empty, exhausted, and impoverished. Fair is fair; those who live by the imaginary
sword must die a slow death from the pinpricks of
misfortune.

Debt and Greed

As a symbol of greed and an object of dread, consider
the monster at the heart of the labyrinth designed by
Daedalus. Half man, half bull, the Minotaur was the
child of an insatiable desire. Pasiphaë, King Minos's
queen, had so desired to have intercourse with a certain
pure white bull that she asked Daedalus to build a fac-
simile of a cow for her. Her plan was to place herself
advantageously within the cow and to receive the bull;
the ingenious deception worked, and she gave birth to
the monster Minotaur. The labyrinth, like the fake cow,
was itself both deceptive and ingenious, designed by
Daedalus to conceal the monster from public view. This
creation of Daedalus was indeed a complex designed to
cover and satisfy greed. Like the psychoanalytic image of
the primitive self of the child, the monster ingests, chews
up, swallows, and eliminates its personal environment.
The myth has it that young men and women were brought
from Greece to be consumed by the Minotaur, just as
Minos himself was destroying the youth of Athens in the

maritime wars. Nonetheless, the myth points beyond Minos to the greed that underlies all social institutions. Any consuming passion is, by definition, destructive. That is why, in the myth, greed has to be concealed by such elaborate and complex handiwork as a labyrinth. If it were widely understood that the heart of social life is an all-consuming passion, individuals would justifiably live in dread.

Greed begets debt, a debt that cannot be paid no matter how many young people are sacrificed or how much money or time is wasted. No matter how cleverly one finds one's way through the complex pathways that a society devises to conceal and yet satisfy this consuming passion, there is no way to satisfy the debt itself. Count up the sacrifices, the goods consumed and destroyed by the pursuit of whatever symbolic rewards a society has to offer; in the end, there is no way to satisfy this monstrous hunger for more payments. At least, as the year 2000 approaches, the end of the game has not yet appeared in sight.

This greed has two faces. One is the face of social institutions: hard, smooth granite, like the temples in which sacrifices were made or like the walls of Daedalus's labyrinth. Speaking of that labyrinth and its maker, Ovid describes Daedalus as

> . . . an artist
> Famous in building, who could set in stone
> Confusion and conflict, and deceive the eye
> With devious aisles and passages.
> —Ovid 1955: Book VIII, ll. 161–164

There is something infinitely complex and tortuous about the social pathways that lead the young to the places where their various lives are demanded of them; that may well have been Ovid's point.

On the other hand, however, destructive emotion can

be personified in the individual, notably in public officials or heroes. Campbell (1972:15) notes that King Minos had started the tragedy of the Minotaur by making an
improper sacrifice to Poseidon. Such flawed performance of ritual fails to satisfy the debt. In Minos's case,
the debt to Poseidon was for enriching the maritime
kingdom of Crete. Poseidon personified his favor to Minos in the gift of a pure white bull, which Minos was
commanded to offer in sacrifice to the god in payment of
his enormous debt. Instead of returning the bull to Poseidon in sacrifice, however, Minos kept it for himself
and substituted another. It was Poseidon's bull that had
charmed the queen, Pasiphaë, and that had sired the
monster, the Minotaur. The symbol of greed, the insatiable Minotaur, was therefore the offspring not only of the
queen's lust but also of the king's own greed in holding
back for himself what had been due Poseidon. Those
who do not lend themselves fully to rituals in which
they appear to dedicate themselves to public service
thereby incur a debt for which they pay dearly.

If it is institutionalized greed that calls for the sacrifice of one generation after another, it is the greed of
rulers that makes them unwilling to give themselves
wholly to the rites of their office. Joseph Campbell puts
it this way:

> Thus according to ancient legend, the primary fault was not
> the queen's lust but the king's; and he could not really
> blame her, for he knew what he had done. He had con-
> verted a public event to personal gain, whereas his whole
> sense of his investiture as king had been that he was no
> longer a mere private person. The return of the bull should
> have symbolized his absolutely selfless submission to the
> functions of his role. The retaining of it represented, on the
> one hand, an impulse to egocentric self-aggrandizement.
> And so the king "by the grace of God" became the danger-
> ous tyrant Holdfast—out for himself. Just as the traditional
> rites of passage used to teach the individual to die to the

past and be reborn to the future, so the great ceremonials
of investiture divested him of his private character and
clothed him in the mantle of his vocation. Such was the
ideal, whether the man was a craftsman or a king. By the
sacrilege of the refusal of the rite, however, the individual
cut himself as a unit off from the larger unit of the whole
community: and so the One was broken into the many, and
these then battled each other—each out for himself—and
could be governed only by force. (1972:15)

At the heart of the myth, then, is the unpaid debt: a debt
to the gods who alone have the right to demand payment
of one's life in full. It is as if a ritual were a symbolic and
magical way of discharging the debt to the greed that
underlies all of social life.

Ritual, however, is a thin line of defense against
greedy and destructive impulses. That is why rites have
to be observed with such care. The slightest inattention
to detail can produce quite dangerous results. In the
days prior to recent revisions of the Anglican *Book of
Common Prayer,* for instance, the faithful would be
invited to Holy Communion with a solemn warning
against coming without proper spiritual preparation.
Those who greedily consume the wine and the wafer
without discerning their true spiritual meaning incur
their own destruction. The kernel of truth in the warning, which has been dropped entirely from current usage, is that ritual in traditional societies was a primary
means of satisfying and paying off the debt to the deepest levels of psychological greed, that innermost hunger
of the soul for total consumption of the means of life.
Left unsatisfied, greed can wreak havoc. Left uncon-
trolled by the proper observance of ritual, the debt to
greed must be paid by others. It is often paid by those
who have the least to give—by the helpless and vulnerable members of a society.

The ritual turns such excessive desire into a surplus of
devotion. The ritualized reaction against destructive

greed is especially important in the rites of passage to which Campbell referred in the passage I have just quoted. One such rite, of course, commemorates the passage from citizen to public official, as in the anointing of a king. Another such rite, however, comes with adolescence, when the young seek to take on the authority—and take over the positions—of their elders. It is a time when greedy emotions can be terribly destructive to both the young and the old. The old, fearful of being replaced and hungry for the energies of the young, can demand terrible sacrifices. The stories told by Ovid are full of the slaying of the young by their fathers and sometimes even by their mothers. But the danger of filicide is matched by the danger of parricide. Certainly Icarus seems to want to outshine and supersede his father. The point is simply that greed, an insatiable hunger to consume all the sources of spiritual power and vital energy, is the source of a debt that must be paid and transformed in ritual if it is not to be satisfied by bloodier sacrifices.

One trouble with ritual is that it so often fails; that is why it has to be repeated over and over again. It was this repetition that fascinated Freud, who found in his patients a desire to repeat the same words or gestures as if to be reassured of their magical effect; yet the reassurance was never enough to quiet their minds once and for all.

It is as if the observance of a rite is meant to prevent something terrible from happening—an outburst of destructive passion or all-consuming rage. "Enough" is never quite "enough" when the debt to be satisfied is owed to an insatiable hunger in the soul.

Remember that one of the ways that a consuming passion can express itself is in a fear of being drained. The logic of the unconscious is simple and somewhat literal minded, going something like this: "I am a greedy organism; therefore the world also is greedy and might consume me. I can drain the world of its energies; therefore I might also be drained by the greed of others. The punishment fits the crime (Freud's *lex talionis*); therefore it is right as well as predictable that others will do to me as I—at least in my imagination—have done to them. Q.E.D.: I can expect that my own resources will be drained by others. They are finite and cannot easily be renewed or restored. I am in danger of being sucked dry."

It is understandable, then, to feel that one's own cultural resources have been drained or emptied of their power. An anthropologist might speak of "cultural exhaustion": the feeling of a people that their beliefs or rituals have lost their vitality and no longer can guarantee the safety or well-being of the community. The magic goes out of people's faith; its institutions seem powerless to save. The crops are meager; the young pay no respect to their elders. A nation develops concern over its defenses or over the scholastic achievements of the young. Some fear a "brain drain," from the loss of ability to competing nations. There may be fear over the flight of capital or the exhaustion of certain natural resources. At such times a people may seek to pay a debt to the ancestors, enshrine its founding documents, celebrate the virtues of an important national statue, and find other means of restoring what they feel has been drained from the country's reserves. Daedalus sacrificed to Apollo after Icarus had spent himself in futile flight.

The nation-state has the most to lose from a widespread feeling of cultural exhaustion. Its own legitimacy depends on the credit borrowed from reserves stored in the family or the countryside, in neighborhoods or religious communities. The state lives on borrowed authority and drains what it can from a nation's resources of people and energy, of spiritual commitments and financial reserves. During a period of cultural exhaustion the state, as in the Soviet Union and other Eastern Bloc countries, seeks to revive the churches, rehabilitates scien-

tists who have been neglected or imprisoned, finds
spiritual wisdom in the people's piety previously ignored or deplored, and makes concessions to ethnic or
regional loyalties. To restore what it has drained away
becomes an obligation the state cannot leave unpaid if it
wishes to survive.

The greedier the institution, the more it must restore
what it has taken; otherwise it will run out of recruits
and raw materials. It is the function of a certain class of
intellectuals to find such new machinery for the state: to
devise new techniques for education, new technologies,
new ways of motivating the young to participate in the
sacrifices called for by the state. The discovery that only
a minority of draftees could pass the selective service
examination, while the remainder were physically or in-
tellectually below standard, motivated strenuous efforts
in the 1960s to upgrade the United States' school system
and to make sure that the nation's young were physically
fit. The fitness slogans of the period did not explicitly
refer to the selective service; the question of "fit for
what" was not raised on the back of cold cereal boxes,
except to infer that one might run or throw better if one
were eating the same cereal as the pictured athlete. It
became public policy to restore the energies of an earlier era, when the young were more vigorous, mentally
alert, and, presumably, readier to serve.

In antiquity the class of intellectuals whose job it was
to innovate was the *daedaloi*. Daedalus himself developed a complex new machinery for the recruitment and
sacrifice of young men and women: the labyrinth. Their
energies were consumed by the Minotaur, but the invention of the labyrinth also served to hide the greed and
destructiveness at the heart of the designs of King Minos.
Those designs were to consume as much of Greece and
the neighboring islands as possible. What we have in
this myth, in part at least, is the recognition that com-
plexity serves the purpose of the state, which is to domi-

nate and to consume as much of the energies of its people and of adjacent lands as possible. Those designs are furthered by the complex constructions of the daedaloi: the innovators whose skills serve the most powerful institutions of their societies.

The daedaloi were innovators in one sense; they fashioned new instruments of domination. Daedalus was a craftsman, a sculptor, an inventor. Nonetheless, even at the moment in which he was most innovative and inventive, Daedalus was also serving the dominant institutions of his day. In the invention of the labyrinth, Daedalus served the purposes of the state. In the invention of the wings that fashioned their escape from the island, Daedalus was serving the purpose of patriarchal authority. That purpose is to ensure that the younger generations stay within the limits prescribed by their elders. The task of patriarchal authority is also its primary dilemma: to find a new generation of successors who are willing to stay within the limits set by the older generation while acquiring the powers of the elders. Fly neither too high nor too low; either path leads to destruction. The rite of succession is a dangerous one for the elders; they fear the loss of their powers. It is also a dangerous one for the young; not all are found ready or able to make the passage into adulthood. Some perish, like Icarus, along the way.

Underlying the innovation of the wings, then, is an archaic technique for ensuring that the young male will leave behind the most primitive ambition, which is to destroy and replace the father while nonetheless learning to succeed him. The instruction by Daedalus to Icarus is quite literally "Follow me." Only in so doing will the young be found worthy to take the elders' place with a minimum of sacrifice by the fathers. Paradoxically, the innovation of Daedalus is really in the service of a traditional institution, patriarchy, and relies on a very traditional means of passing authority and instruction from one generation to the next, a rite of passage that, in the myth, is disguised as a flight heavenward through dangers from above and below. In the Daedalus myth, the class of innovators, the daedaloi, not only serves the interest of the state but also perpetuates the dominance of fathers over sons.

The myth conceals another paradox of domination, that the dominated must learn to love their subordination and to experience it as an accomplishment of their own. Joseph Campbell (1972:136–137), writing of the rites of male initiation in a wide range of tribes, describes the psychological process that the young male must pass through if he is to be considered competent to take on the role of father, to be (like Daedalus) a spiritual guide: "The mystagogue (father or father-substitute) is to entrust the symbols of office only to a son who has been effectually purged of all . . . unconscious (or perhaps even conscious and rationalized) motives of self-aggrandizement, personal preference, or resentment" (1972:136).

It is therefore not surprising that patriarchal ideology seeks to disguise this inner contradiction in its rites and ideology. The ideology of patriarchal authority, Weber reminded us, claims that the life of the community depends on the ministries and authority of the patriarchs. It is they who manage conflict, guarantee the smooth flow of goods and money, defend the community from its enemies, and ensure the fertility of the fields. Life itself depends on patriarchal authority; that is the claim. In a nutshell, the creation itself is restored by the patriarchs. Of course they demand sacrifice, because it is through sacrifice that life is passed on from one generation to the next.

A few examples may make the point clearer. Joseph Campbell recounts how Australian aborigines both intimidate and succor young males seeking admission to adulthood; the young, first terrified by drums and threats of disaster, are then urged to drink the blood offered them by their mother's brothers (1972:139ff.). A number of myths, Campbell notes, show the male god of life as the twin of the male god of death. Indeed, a prehistoric father-god (Peruvian or Argentinean) sheds tears in the form of "the rains that refresh the life of the valleys of the world" (1972:145). It is in this vein that we are to understand, I would suggest, the similar tears shed by Daedalus as he sought to prepare his son Icarus for flight:

> And now to fit the wings to the boy's shoulders.
> Between the work and warning the father found
> His cheeks were wet with tears, and his hands trembled.
> He kissed his son (*Goodbye,* if he had known it),
> Rose on his wings, flew on ahead, as fearful
> As any bird launching the little nestlings
> Out of a high nest into thin air.
> —Ovid 1955: Book VIII, ll. 209–215

How are we to interpret these tears? I have already suggested that there is some guilty knowledge at work in these rites of passage. The older generation knows that it is curing the debt it owes to the world by passing that debt on to the next generation. The tears may be evidence of some guilt. The older generation may be taking some satisfaction in the sufferings imposed on the younger generation, especially if there are residues of greed and of strivings for domination that remain in the fathers' hearts; the tears may be like those of the crocodile in the fairy story as it contemplates its future victims. The tears may also reflect a sense of tragedy, as the older generation contemplates the cost of restoring a world that has been depleted by its own and past generations' greed and destructiveness. Daedalus must know, of course, about the sacrifices to the Minotaur who was born with his own connivance. Daedalus had built, after all, the cow that had covered queen Pasiphaë and deceived the white bull, whose issue was the Minotaur. Daedalus is thus initiating his son into a world whose demands for sacrifice have to be met through his own craft and ingenuity. The war memorial to the young students killed in an anti-Vietnam War demonstration at Kent State University in Ohio during 1968 makes the point very well; it shows Isaac kneeling at his father's feet, and Abraham holding the knife to his son's throat. There is guilty and possibly remorseful knowledge at work in this myth, as well as possibly some secret satisfaction.

The tears of the patriarch found in the Daedalus and other myths therefore have several interpretations. It is relatively obvious that the tears represent the paradoxes and conflicts of patriarchal authority. One such paradox is that in promising life the patriarch calls for the sacrifice of the life of some in the next generation. A similar paradox contrasts the patriarchal promise of liberty with the demand for constraint. Thus the patriarchal claim to restore the world and to keep it moving, is contradicted by the legacy of death that the older generation passes to the young—death as a payment for liberties taken and for grandiose claims to power and satisfaction. While paying the debt of their generation to a society or culture that they have used, drained, or even exhausted, the older generation creates a new generation with unsatisfied and unsatisfiable claims on the world. It is the task of the older generation to make sure that the next generation does not exhaust the world or defeat itself in making demands impossible to satisfy. In fulfilling that task, the patriarch demands the sacrifice of the sons' desires for power and satisfaction, lest the world be consumed by their desires. In the end, Phoebus, the sun god, has to watch while his son Phaeton is destroyed by a thunderbolt from Jove; otherwise the whole creation would have gone up in the flames caused by the chariot of fire as it went out of control, scorched the heavens, and literally reduced the earth to ashes. To preserve life, the fathers have to acquiesce in the slaughter of their sons. If this seems esoteric, consider the feelings of parents who offer their sons for military service. There are causes for parental, and not only patriarchal, tears in this call to duty. Certainly the fates of Icarus and Perdix point in the direction of punishment for such rivalry.

Here I wish to explore further the debt that is owed the creation, the world, by each generation. It is the task of each generation to renew the world that has nourished it and to restore the energies that have been drained from the breast of Mother Earth. To pay this debt, however, is far beyond the capacities of mere men and their phalluses. What is the seed without the earth, the phallus without the womb? Somehow, if the patriarchal ideology is to deliver on its promise of renewing and sustaining life in the world, it is important for men to usurp the powers of women. As Campbell points out, that is just what Zeus promises to his son:

Come, O Dithyrambos,
Enter this my male womb.
   —Euripides, *The Bacchae,* quoted in Campbell 1972

The Dithyramb, Campbell (1972) notes, is an epithet for the one who is born again. While it applies to Dionysus, the name also refers to the songs sung in chorus in the rites that promised the renewal of fertility and of the cosmos in each new season. To fulfill its promise of restoring the world, the patriarch must become both man and woman, phallus and womb, the place and the means of generation.

Women, then, are virtually eliminated from the patriarchal ideology, as men replace them. That is entirely obvious to women who seek ordination in the most patriarchal churches, even in the late 1900s. The resistance to women, however rationalized on theological grounds, derives from the fundamental attempt by pa-

triarchs to eliminate and replace women by their own
dramatic performances. The ceremonial commanded by
male clergy, from rites of immersion in water with
promise of a new birth to rites that promise new life
from bread and wine, are dramatizations of the claim
that males can and do possess full control over the
means of birth and life itself. Women are not needed or
wanted in such performances; their presence would give
the lie to the claims of men to have embodied the womb
along with the phallus.

More is at stake here, of course, than the ideology of
patriarchal authority or the attempt by one gender to
upstage the other. At issue is the claim to be able to
create oneself and remake the world through magically
potent words and gestures. Remember that the greedy
self, the inner Pac-Man, so to speak, wishes to be able to
guarantee its life by consuming all that there is. The
desire is to be all-in-all: in total possession of the means
of life and therefore self-sustaining. It is the same desire
that produces the sense of indebtedness to the world
that has been consumed by this boundless passion. The
passion, in other words, knows no bounds. That is why
Daedalus insisted that while Minos might have him con-
tained on the island surrounded by the sea, the air remained open. The command of the powers of flight has
its roots, then, in the desire to create one's self and to
possess heaven on earth.

In the desire to possess heaven on earth, however, the
male must consume the female and subsume her life-
giving powers. Campbell (1972:149ff.) notes that many
cultures describe the human archetype as androgynous.
The image of God contains both the male and the female, according to one of the Genesis myths of creation.
In psychoanalytic terms, the grandiose imagination of
the infant inflates himself or herself into one all-
encompassing being that can swallow up even time into
eternity.

There are rites of initiation that act out this desire to create an all-encompassing, androgynous, and self-sustaining man, and Campbell (1972:154–155) mentions that one is particularly useful for understanding the Daedalus myth. Remember Campbell's description of the Australian aborigines' rites of initiation. It seems that a year after this rigorous initiation the young men find their penises under attack once again, this time not for circumcision but for subincision. The cut is made beneath the penis to symbolize the opening to the womb. From it, according to Australian belief, flow a variety of life-giving or nutrient fluids. At this time the older men paint the youths' bodies and glue upon them the down of white birds. Think of Ovid's account here of Icarus, who

> Stood by and watched [Daedalus],
> Not knowing he was dealing with his downfall,
> Stood by and watched, and raised his shiny face
> To let a feather, light as down, fall on it
> Or stuck his thumb into the yellow wax,
> Fooling around, the way a boy will, always,
> Whenever a father tries to get some work done.
> —Ovid 1955: Book VIII, ll. 183ff.

Perhaps there are reminiscences here of an initiation involving downy feathers, in which a son learns the ways of the father and enters the mystery of male dominance over the elements, like the bird who soars heavenward. Although the myth speaks of wax and twine as the elements binding the feathers to the body, rather than the blood from a wounded penis, the point is that a rite of male initiation may be taking place, which excludes women while enabling a boy to transcend the boundaries of gender. As Campbell puts it, "The hero has become, by virtue of the ceremonial, more than man. . . . The flowing of blood . . . shows that the old men have the source of life and nourishment within themselves; i.e., that they and the inexhaustible world fountain are the same" (1972:155).

One purpose of the rite of passage that may underlie the Daedalus myth is therefore to purge the world of greedy motives and to restore the creation. To make the world anew, to restore the creation, is the task of innovators. Whether sculptors, artisans, or inventors, they seek to restore what greed has destroyed—to make the world new again. The paradox, that they must restore the creation by perpetuating the dominance of old institutions over the young, is part of what I mean by the term "the Daedalus complex." The debt to the world is simply recycled to the next generation, who may demand satisfaction for their sacrifices or refuse to honor the debt left unpaid by the previous generation.

That is one reason why the rite of passage into the adult world seeks to purge acquisitiveness from the souls of the young. There are sacrifices to be made, and the old do not wish to pay the bill for the losses incurred by the young. That is why the rite must promise unprecedented liberty, a soaring to new heights, and at the same time instill respect for the limits imposed by the fathers on the sons. In the name of restoring the creation, therefore, rites of passage perpetuate resentment at sacrifice and at the inevitable frustration of the deepest and most intractable hunger for life and power.

Rites of initiation often emphasize the restoration of the created world, the natural universe and its seasonal order. The same rites that bring young men into the company of an older age grouping may also drive away sickness and bring healing to the world; so was Apollo honored in initiation rites in Crete (Burkert 1985:145). On Crete young men were initiated in rites honoring Zeus; these rituals also combined the advancement of boys to a higher status (as young warriors), with invocations for a new year filled with divine blessings. The restoration of the natural order, in each new year, seems to require the sacrifice of the young to a god who remains distant, powerful, and capable of bringing terrible bane as well as blessing. As a society renews itself with each new generation, the universe is renewed by the god who, like Apollo, can bring both plague and healing (Burkert 1985:145–146).

Dread and the Failure of Ritual

There remains, however, the question of whether the rite has succeeded or failed in requiring the death of Icarus. Perhaps the myth recalls ancient sacrifices of the young to guarantee the renewal of both nature and society. There is some warrant for thinking that the Daedalus myth recalls the sacrifice of the young. Burkert (1985:63) notes that the *daedala* were "rude, human-shaped idols made of wood"; these were offered in fire rituals by the Boeotians on Mount Kithairon. In another discussion of the same rite, Burkert (1979:132–143) goes on to describe how these wooden images were consumed by fire in a celebration of the renewal of fertility, through the mating of Earth and Sky and the ending of all drought and illness. Elsewhere, however, Burkert (1985:26–28) expands his description of the fire festivals to include celebrations on mountain peaks in Minoa, primarily from about 2000 to 1500 B.C.E.; these were the forerunners of the fire celebrations at which the wooden idols, the daedala, were burned. At these earlier, Minoan rites a wide range of idols was consumed by fire, many of them molded from clay, and at some rites there may well have been human sacrifice. It is likely that the myth of Daedalus reflects this belief that renewal of the creation or even just the healing of the sick requires the giving of life, if in return life is to be given by the gods. In modern societies, the call is for the individual to be sacrificed.

The same hint of human sacrifice lends a darker dimension to the fate of Icarus and would explain the apprehension and dread of Daedalus. If that tragic flight is suddenly interrupted by his death, that too fits the description of a "Cretan sacrifice" (Burkert 1985:27), which ends suddenly and dramatically, as though something terrible has happened. Indeed it has: "Again and again, the sacrifice of a man or of a god, hinted at in ritual and executed in myth, lies behind the fire festivals" (Burkert 1985:63). The sense that a terrible payment must be made to guarantee the renewal of life haunts Greek mythology; there are indeed sacrifices to be made, at times gruesome ones.

The narcissistic withdrawal of self-love from its sublimation in the community requires that life itself be given back, from one year to the next, to guarantee the renewal of the community's ideal self. The *lex talionis,* as Freud reminded us, is also the logic of the unconscious: an eye for an eye and a tooth for a tooth. In the rivalry between generations, moreover, there is more than a hint of mortal combat. Especially in the rites that usher in a new year through the initiation of a new age group, there is often more than a hint of sacrificial killing. *Where nature and society die and are renewed in the same rites, the experience of dread over the measure of the debt to be paid may be the most intense.* In modern societies, where nature and society are more differentiated, such dread is more chronic than intense.

In rites that celebrate the end of one year at the beginning of the next, there are ample reminiscences of death: the death of the old order, of the old calendar, of the vegetation and the fertility of the fields, and even of an age. The transition from one year to the next, like many other transitions, is experienced and translated in myth as a dying and a new birth. That much is clear from Burkert's analyses of new year festivals and their attendant sacrifices. Why, however, should such celebrations give rise to what Burkert (1985:231) calls "an unsettling atmosphere of guilt"? Is the slaughter of a bull so disastrous that individuals seek to flee from the scene of

the crime? Burkert (1985:231) argues that "the terrible-
ness of the destruction of life is demonstrated in the
ritus"; somehow, if everyone reenacts the apparent
crime, the burden of guilt for having absorbed so much
life is distributed in a way that makes the burden light.

To pay for the restoration of the created, natural, and
social order is indeed a heavy duty. That is, in part, no
doubt why tribes and city-states, Athens included, allowed the most subordinate and oppressed elements of
the population relatively free play in the final month of
the year. It was then that the slaves of Athens ran
through the streets and the women gathered in their
assemblies to denounce the men (Burkert 1985:231–
232). In these symbolic payments the community
sought to restore what it had taken and to make possible
a year of renewed sacrifice and obedience on the part of
the dispossessed.

Another source of dread can be found in rites of annual renewal that are associated with rites of initiation.
In the myth of Daedalus and Icarus, as I have suggested,
there may be traces of such rites of initiation; certainly
there is the suggestion of an arduous passage on which
the old lead the young through danger to safety. Icarus
perishes, albeit because of his own failure to follow directions and accept the limits imposed by the older generation. Later in the myth Perdix, Daedalus's nephew, is
actually pushed by his jealous uncle from the top of a
tower.

The myth pits the sun against the sea: Apollo against
Poseidon. It is the task of each generation successfully to
navigate between the sea and sky, between the heights
and the depths, and to avoid the dangers of excess in
either direction. In some ritual contexts, according to
Burkert (1985:221–222), the sea may represent an "el-
emental force" and be opposed to "technical wisdom";
in other rites the sea may represent the old as opposed
to the young: "watery depths" versus "youthful vigor."

Poseidon and Apollo, or Poseidon and Athena: the po-
larities vary from one myth to another. What is at stake,
however, is the conflict of one generation with another
and their mutual need for each other. That conflict, as
Freud reminded us, is the source of ambivalence, of unconscious desires to murder each other, and of an intense sense of having an unfulfilled debt to be paid.

Often the unconscious debt is paid at the expense of
one's own life. Icarus pays with his life for his excesses;
Perdix is sacrificed, only to be saved by Minerva. The
latent conflict in rites of initiation is murderous, and the
sacrifices are dear, unless the two generations, like
Apollo and Poseidon, "encounter each other with
respect and avoid entering into conflict" (Burkert
1985:222).

Another detail of the Daedalus myth suggests that the
relationship of the two generations could indeed be ben-
eficial. In the Perdix version, Daedalus is an uncle. As
Burkert notes, "the implied uncle or patron relationship may ultimately be connected with initiations"
(1985:222). The point is that a younger generation represents a terrible threat to the older age group, and that
the distance between the two, like the distance between
sea and the sky, must be traversed with care, delibera-
tion, and respect for the leadership of the old. Otherwise, there may be a terrible fall, and the young may
perish.

Faced with the task of renewing their societies and
their natural environments, the older generation requires that the next generation pay its share of the debt
of restoration. The unfulfilled obligations of the older
generation are thus passed on to the young; hence the
need for the young to sacrifice a measure of their own
dreams of domination and satisfaction. Through the
Daedalus complex the debt not only to maintain but to
restore what one generation has consumed or destroyed
is therefore passed on to the next generation in the most

solemn of rites. Their solemnity is designed to ensure that the young will sacrifice their own greed, their own self-love, or invest that love in the ideals of the community and the society. Indeed, as Freud argued, the sense that one has withdrawn self-love from its sublimated form in the larger society and recovered that love for oneself, compounds the sense of debt. It is as if one is afraid that the society, like a parent from whom one withdraws love, would return the insult with a mortal injury. One lives in mortal dread of such retaliation for love withdrawn from the source of one's life.

Rites of initiation, therefore, inspire dread to the extent that they compound the debt of the older generation with the debt of the younger age group: the debt to restore the society with the debt owed to a community from which self-love has been withdrawn. If Daedalus owes the society recompense for the destruction caused by his handiwork, Icarus owes the society recompense for the love withheld as he plays and impedes the work of his father. It is the interaction between the greed of one generation and the self-love of the other that underlies this aspect of the Daedalus complex. In modern societies rites of initiation are unable to inspire such dread. As a result, dread becomes free-floating, as do greed and guilt, rather than being focused in specific rites.

Clearly, no one, not even fathers, has within himself or herself the means of renewing his or her own and others' lives. It is make-believe in the most serious sense to engage in such rites. Of course, the gestures are meant to create faith in others and in oneself: faith that one can magically guarantee the sources of one's own life by being both mother and father and by being an obedient child. Such make-believe is clearly a delusion.

No doubt the Daedalus complex originates in the unconscious, where profound wishes supported by the magical thinking of infancy continue to dominate the thoughts and practices of many adults, especially in the spheres of life considered sacred. No matter how deeply one is committed to certain rituals, no matter how solemnly one covers the body with white down from the feathers of sacred birds, one can never sustain one's own life forever. Indeed, the therapeutic values of psychoanalysis depend largely on confronting such magical thinking and the wishes for eternal life that sustain it. They confront the fact that one cannot guarantee for oneself or for anyone else an inexhaustible supply of vitality or of life itself.

Psychoanalysis has no monopoly on this criticism of the sacred. The myth of the Fall in Genesis contains precisely such a warning against the desire to fill oneself with the sources of unending life. It is permitted to Adam and Eve neither to be omniscient nor to have access to unending life. Those fruits grow on a tree that is forbidden. Like Daedalus and Icarus, Adam and Eve make demands on life that the created world is unable to fulfill; they are still held captive by the wishful thinking and insatiable desires of infancy for magical control over the sources of life.

Indeed, there are several analogies between the Daedalus myth and the myth of the Fall. The punishment for seeking to control the sources of life is death, in both the myths. Ovid speaks of the contrivance of flying as a "fatal art" (Ovid 1955: Book VIII, 1. 217); the fall of Icarus is immanent in the inventiveness and craft of Daedalus. It is as if culture (the knowledge of good and evil or of the means to sustain life) were in itself a "fatal art" designed to prevent the very tragedy that it inevitably causes in those who rely on their own inventiveness. The myth implies a critique of all culture, insofar as culture arises from the primitive narcissism of the infant who seeks magical access and control over life itself. The implication of both myths is that these wishes, translated into technology, are motivated by a desire to be like God; as Daedalus and Icarus fly overhead, the fisherman, the shepherd, and the ploughman

> . . . all look up, in absolute amazement,
> At those air-borne above. They must be gods!
> —Ovid 1955: Book VIII, ll. 223–224

If there is one rule for understanding myth, it is that the punishment suffered by the god or hero fits the crime. Along with Freud, Reik (1957; 1970) is perhaps the most insistent on this point. Christ suffers incorporation into the tree (the cross) because he is being punished for the primal crime in which the father-god, worshiped as a tree, was consumed by humans (cf. Reik 1970:297ff.). The primal crime is the slaying of the father-god, but in its most regressed form the crime is one of consumption; one slays what one eats, because there is nothing left. Although Reik is contemptuous of explanations that fix on the infant's relation to the mother, he does admit that the most primitive passions, the greedy desire to consume and destroy the sources of life, are at the heart of Greek, Jewish, and Christian myth. Incorporation, being swallowed up into the tree or into God himself, is the punishment for the primal crime of destructive consumption of the sources of life.

It is sometimes not so easy to see the relation of the punishment to the crime. In the case of Daedalus, for instance, the problem is especially complicated by the fact that there are two parts to the myth. In the first part, Daedalus loses Icarus because Icarus seeks to transcend his father and rise inappropriately to the heights. The son's desire to eclipse the father in this way leads, on the face of it, to the death of the son: a simple *quid pro quo*. Myths, like dreams, however, have more than one level of meaning, many significant details, and therefore multiple interpretations. Especially when it is difficult to assign the myth to a specific time or place in history, it is difficult to distinguish the primary from the secondary

aspects of myth. Nonetheless, it is clear that in the first
part of the myth it is Daedalus who is suffering through
the loss of his son. It is he who pays the penalty; in the
end of the first part, therefore, Daedalus makes the sacrifice to Apollo. The transgression would seem to have
been Daedalus's desire to have been like the gods; birds,
after all, were symbols or representations of the gods. In
this sense, the punishment fits the crime through a reversal of fortunes; the man who seeks to transcend the
father-god loses his own son.

The notion that a punishment can be reversed to fit
a crime backward, so to speak, is not unusual. Reik
(1970:274) argues that the sacrifice of Isaac by Abraham is just such a reversed punishment for the crime of
trying to turn the tables on God, in which the son takes
the place of the father. The rebellious son loses his son
(Isaac, Icarus), as it were; it is a theme that Freud finds
in literature and in the theater, notably the Macbeth
saga. The crime of Daedalus, like that of Sisyphus (cf.
Reik 1970:295), is that he was too crafty; his inventions
stole the prerogatives of the gods to be the source of
innovation and creativity. Sisyphus, who sought to build
a monument to himself, a city set upon a hill, finds that
he is condemned to roll a stone uphill for eternity.
Daedalus, equally crafty in building a labyrinth in which
the young of Athens were to be sacrificed to the Minotaur, also is condemned to lose his son: an eye for an
eye. Masochism thus becomes a way of life for Sisyphus;
for Daedalus the loss of Icarus is not sufficient payment,
so that further sacrifice is required.

To put it another way: The aggression of humans toward their parents can be carried out, from one generation to the next, in aggression against their children. The
origins of child abuse lie in the childhood of the parent,
who may well have been abused as a child and have
wished to triumph over, even to kill, a hated parent. The
reversal of which Reik speaks is not only a trick of the

unconscious or an element in myth; it is acted out daily in the lives of thousands of parents and children. In other words, fantasies of triumph over the parent may be rooted in real sufferings rather than in the grandiose imagination of the infant, who imagines the world to be its oyster. Whether the object of aggression is the parent or whether that aggression is displaced onto the next generation, that is, to one's own children, the problem is the same: how to keep the drive toward power and vengeance from becoming chronic, a masochistic way of life.

The Daedalus complex, then, reflects a masochism that is social; that is, the sufferings are chronic, enduring, and intended to deprive both generations of the satisfaction of their own achievements. The second part of the Daedalus myth puts it very simply: Daedalus attacks and seeks to kill his nephew, Perdix. The offense of Perdix, for which Daedalus pushes him from the tower, is that Perdix has become more creative than Daedalus, an inventor in his own right. That is, Perdix has stolen the thunder of the older generation. He represents the very offense for which Daedalus, in the first part of the myth, is punished—transgression against the gods. In the latter half of the myth, therefore, Perdix represents to Daedalus the hated offense; he is not only a threat to Daedalus's authority but also a reminder of the primal sin of individualism, of seeking to be the source and creator of one's own life. To be one's own inventor is to steal from the tree of life. The punishment for the self-invented individual, in the Eden myth and in the story of Perdix or Icarus, is death.

If this seems too harsh an interpretation of poor Perdix's offense, remember that he is rescued in the end by the mother figure, the goddess Minerva, who shelters him and gives him wings. It is not an insignificant detail. In fact, it puts the myth in the company of other myths in which the suffering son is raised to exclusive heights

to take the place of the father after suffering for his transgression against the father (cf. Reik 1970:302).

The Surplus of Indebtedness

There is a surplus of indebtedness in any society, de-
riving from unfulfilled desires of every sort. In this chapter I have focused on the desire to restore the creation,
to give back what one has received, and to rescue those
who are in danger of sickness and death. To make an
offering may have served all of these purposes at once:
to restore and to rescue, to recover and to save. At the
same time, such offerings may have signified the offering
of a new age group to the society as a down payment on
the promise of each generation to pay its way in life.
Fathers offered sons, and the young lent themselves, to
the task of redeeming the debt to life.

Social life emerged, then, as a way of absorbing this
surplus of devotion, of unfulfilled desire. Every year the
annual rites of restoring creation had to be repeated. The
remains of old votive offerings were swept aside. A new
holocaust of burnt offerings lit fires on mountain peaks,
sacred altars, temple shrines. To satisfy these overwhelming desires for well-being, it was necessary to
transform them into devotions and to provide priests and
sacred places, calendars and sacred rites. In addition, it
was necessary to have a way of distributing the surplus
not consumed by the sacred fires: animals and gifts of
various sorts, precious or earthen. A small class of artisans and craftsmen supported themselves by fashioning
the daedala, not to mention the commerce that flour-
ished around the central sacred places. Even as late as
the first century C.E., the Palestinian economy depended
largely on pilgrimages to Jerusalem and the sacrifices
offered at the Temple there. When the Temple was destroyed and the city burned in the civil war of 66–70

C.E., the economy of the countryside as well as of the city disintegrated.

Of course, the central shrines of any society, even in antiquity, lacked a monopoly on such devotions. I have already suggested that unfulfilled desire was often turned into duty and debt at the grave site, where some of the most costly and extravagant offerings were made. It may well be that the Daedalus myth also includes a reminiscence of funeral rites and the danger of insufficient payment of debts to the dead. The point is that traditional societies developed according to their inventions for absorbing the debt that overflowed from one generation to the next and from the living to the dead.

Those early social inventions were largely rites, the institutions and personnel that performed them, and the devotees and those who provided for them. The votive offerings mentioned in this chapter were therefore both corporate and highly personal. They were corporate because they were the act of an entire community, gathered at sacred times and places for sacred purposes. The personal desires of each individual may have been transformed into a sense of specific obligation, for example, to cure a child, heal a diseased limb or organ, or complete a singular journey. The desire to take advantage of a particular opportunity, to make a visit, or to prevent disaster thus had very specific variations, but the theme was often generic. In the end, despite the singular quality of each prayer for renewal or safety, for healing or redemption, one votive offering looked very much like another. On the surface, it would appear that such traditional societies were very adept at translating the surplus of individual desire into a debt that could only be paid to the chief priests, their servants, and the classes that prospered from the various observances.

However, modern societies have nearly exhausted this surplus of desire-turned-into-debt, this superabundant devotion. The impulse to restore the creation is still highly developed, but it is spent in an extraordinarily wide range of activities other than corporate ceremonies. Science, health, education—these are the names of subsystems within the social system; they are not the names of the gods. The subsystems absorb a huge amount of time and money, work and inspiration. Simply to finance the current programs for health insurance, education, and research in the current federal budget takes months of work by every employed individual. Those who monitor taxes in the United States, in fact, publish the date each year on which average wage earners will begin to work for themselves rather than have their wages garnished for federal, state, and local taxes. Like the tribute offered in traditional societies, these offerings are collected annually. Unlike traditional rites, however, these debts are paid weekly and monthly, in season and out. The institutionalized techniques for transforming desire into debt and for absorbing that debt have far exceeded the episodic, however dramatic, displays of traditional societies.

Modern societies not only have a more diversified and continuous machinery for apprehending the surplus of psychic debt; they also permit individuals far more leeway in choosing their methods of payment. Consider Freud's observation that the obsessive rituals of his patients reminded him of religious rites. The similarities were striking and obvious. Both the patients and the religious devotees were seeking to satisfy some unfulfilled desire by making a payment of some sort in ways that would prevent a disaster and ward off disturbances. Freud also noted, moreover, that much of everyday life resembled the activities of patients that he could observe in his clinic; the mental activities of the "normal" and of the disturbed were not so very different from each other. Instead of "cutting their losses," as it were, individuals with symptoms were paying psychic debts that stood for unfulfilled longings—desires that had been repressed and found expression only in the labyrinthine designs of the unconscious. It is as if everyone has become his or her own Daedalus, innovative in the elaborate construction of channels for transforming desire into obligation.

There is a cost to be paid for this modern form of innovation. Each individual is expected to have unique gifts, to be original, and to find words or gestures that enable his or her personal gift not only to come to light but also to serve some recognizable social purpose. No longer is the virtuoso like Daedalus the only one expected to develop such gifts; the entire society is dedicated to the principle of developing each individual's capacities. The cost to the nation in its educational budget is not the only expense. Some have argued that it is terribly costly to each individual to feel "ordinary." What is often criticized as narcissism, an excessive preoccupation with fulfilling one's potential, is therefore a predictable outcome of social pressures to demonstrate that one has inner resources and can command them effectively in words and deeds. The secularization of the priesthood of all believers makes every individual responsible for offering his or her gifts on the altar of public opinion. That opinion, in the case of the ordinary, can be devastating.

2

The Problem of Debt
and Sacrifice

————➤✠←————

The secularization of the prophetic tradition has pene-
trated the sanctuary of the church itself. For example, it is
paradoxical that the Anglican church, which has main-
tained in its prayer book an antidote to perfectionism and
liberalism with regard to the understanding of sin, has
now decided on both sides of the Atlantic to banish the
phrase "there is no health in us" from its new rites. It is
paradoxical because, as Reinhold Niebuhr (1953:II,
158) points out, it is this phrase that illustrates the
Anglican church's grasp of the prophetic tradition, typifies "the spirit of the prayer of the general confession,"
and explains, along with "the influence of Christian history," why the Anglican tradition's "prayer-book piety"
has been able to resist the secularization that I have been
describing. "At its best," Niebuhr argued, "[the Anglican
church] manages to combine all facets of the Christian
doctrine of grace more truly than other churches,"
(1953:II, 159). Without this phrase and other similar em-
phases on the prophetic understanding of both sin and
grace, the Anglican church resembles Niebuhr's description of Anglicanism: a "compound of liberalistic moralism
and traditional piety" (Niebuhr 1953:II, 159).

The Secularization of Sin:
Beyond the Daedalus Complex

The secularization of the doctrine of sin is paradoxical
in another sense. On both sides of the Atlantic the litur-

gical commissions engaged in revision found various reasons for muting the confession of sin, for example, the "new estates" (suburbs) won't stand for it; it sounds a sour note in the service of baptism to refer to original sin and the possibility of damnation. Times had also changed in America, where the liturgical commission wanted to sound a more triumphal note. The Standing Liturgical Commission of the Episcopal Church, in discussing a traditional petition to save the people of God "from all the perils and dangers of this night," heard that modern amenities had largely expunged the terrors of darkness; the secular city was too well lighted to be a place of terror. The questionable theology and sociology of the time appear paradoxical in their optimism in view of the twentieth century's record of tragedy and disaster; it was just such a record that moved some, in protesting the softening of the sense of sin in the prayer book revision, to call for a more intense expression of sinfulness. These dissenters believed that doctrine, apprehended in faith, precedes "the experience which validates the doctrine"—that is, the experience of "the seriousness of sin" (Niebuhr 1953:II, 120)—and argued that the liturgy should not be determined by current tastes and sensibilities. To paraphrase Niebuhr, one might say that those who had taken neither sin nor history seriously did not realize what has been lost in the liturgical secularization of the doctrine of sin.

The paradox is that in seeking to find a way of speaking that will resonate in the modern ear, the modernizers may well have failed to utter the one word that is most needful to tap the widespread but latent sense of sin that still survives underneath the surfaces of a bureaucratically administered society. To put it in terms of the perennial debate between sociology and pragmatism: The ecclesiastical pragmatists, in their preoccupation with the putative social reality they considered modern, ignored what is both primitive and universal in social life: the propensity to accumulate psychological forms of indebtedness. In this book I will be arguing that the psychological sense of sin is now secularized and takes the form of a residual sense of personal indebtedness either to oneself or to the larger society.

That our understanding of sin depends on the circumstances of our social life is a very basic assumption, and yet one too easily overlooked when we think of sin as a universal and inescapable human propensity for ignoring or confusing ourselves with God. What societies take to be sin is, to put it simply, a social product. The church has clearly lost its monopoly on the production of sin and has been relegated to a relatively minor role, at least in American society. Is it a sin to poison the water supply, falsify information on the dangerous consequences of drugs and chemicals, lie about currency transactions, buy politicians, bomb hospitals on Christmas Day, finance death squads, refuse sanctuary to refugees, or drive whole groups of people to despair? The lack of coherent public discourse and a clear public answer to that question illustrates the gap that has emerged between what this society understands by "spirituality" and the collective actions of an entire nation. There is a vacuum of responsibility caused by the individualistic actions of "corporate actors": the state, corporations, and institutions, and the churches themselves.

That gap, or gulf, allows this society to remain unclear about our collective responsibility for life and death and obscures the question of guilt. There are amenities, presidential pardons, agreements not to contest a decree, and other trivial settlements in public life where more powerful forms of purification and satisfaction were required in earlier societies. It is one thing to describe some aspect of the world, such as nuclear arms, as evil; it is quite another to declare and pronounce it to be anathema to all Christians. The church seems to prefer to describe and recommend, to suggest and to remind, and even occasionally to exhort, rather than to bind and to loose.

In addition, societies form a cultural labyrinth—a complex set of instructions that sacrifice individuals to the interests of certain classes and to corporate actors. For several years, for instance, the public focused on the guilt of Vietnam War veterans: guilty because they have killed, guilty because they may have enjoyed killing, guilty because they have survived while their friends have died for them, and guilty because they have been considered impure by citizens whose hands are relatively clean. Our high culture has produced a literature on the anguish of those who survived. The positive and sensitive work of Lifton not only on veterans of Vietnam but also on the survivors of Hiroshima is a case in point. There has *not* been a commensurate interest in bringing American government officials at the highest levels of government to trial. What used to be a corporate form of sin has been shaped in public discourse into another sort of reality—a personal form of guilt, a human reaction to trauma, a reaction to the loss of social honor, and the experience of being the scapegoat. Such definitions obviously provide certain exemptions to those who initially decided on the carnage; the same definitions also provide employment for those who are professionally trained to listen and respond to sorrow, remorse, and anguish. The people get *The Killing Fields* and *Rambo;* one or two who have the most power either get a pardon or sue the media for libel.

Our actions are savage, but our institutions for dealing with savagery are not primitive or powerful enough to define such suffering and tragedy in terms of collective sin and guilt. Other institutions and other interests, from the entertainment industry to professional counselors, have managed to produce a discourse in which suffering ceases to be sinful in either its cause or effect and calls for no lasting interpretation or judgment. Death loses its power to sting the authorities. The course of secularization, then, makes it very difficult if not impossible for the church to set the terms of public discourse on sin.

In the process of secularization corporate actors become a separate breed from individuals (in their capacity simply as persons rather than as corporate agents). Corporate obligations to the person-as-such become increasingly limited. Each institution elaborates its own rules in a pattern that is consistent with the most general values of the society as a whole, and those values, in turn, allow the individual to take on a limited responsibility and liability determined by job descriptions, professional standards, or public policy. The person-as-such is left to work out his or her own salvation in a way that is either irrelevant to—or at least not consistent with— the values of the larger society. Religion becomes "private" in the sense of not interfering with one's duties. Our society can create new roles, determine their requirements, train and recruit individuals to occupy them, set limits on the roles, provide rewards for adequate performance, and determine when final departure from such roles can be called for. Hiring and firing, educating and retiring, planning and administering, creating and dissolving ties, can be done without "benefit of clergy." The individual *person* is irrelevant, and, I argue, also a victim and scapegoat for the failure of the society itself. "Individualism" becomes the besetting sin of a society in which the "individualists" are not really individuals but corporate actors and their agents.

Some authority is necessary for the construction of roles and for the assignment of certain parts to particular individuals, but performances are a mock trial in which nothing serious appears to be happening. The need to solemnize public discourse on sin or guilt in secular societies is therefore hardly apparent. In simpler societies, of course, individual virtue and spiritual purity often met critical tests of courage and endurance, and these tests were also critical for the individual's own sense of worth and immortality. Tests of prowess in the hunt examined the individual's willingness to risk death in order to provide the sources of life to the human community; they also enabled the individual to overcome the fear of death. So it was with tests of prowess in battle, in leadership, in mating. Simpler societies also provided ways to solemnize the end of life itself, where the last rites posed the final question concerning the individual's motives and intentions and shaped the social meaning of a person's life. Death is always painful and generates passions that may shatter communities and families, estrange parents from children, Jew from Gentile, male from female, and separate people from their own leaders and traditions. Primitive in the passions it generates, it requires the binding of powerful practices and institutions. Death, like life, creates a sense of indebtedness that goes underground in secular societies.

Deaths are not finished until the last word is spoken, and some require more speaking than others. A murder or suicide, for instance, is not done until there is nothing more on the subject to be said or done. Anthropologists (cf. Gluckman 1982) note the ingenious techniques of divination and trial that primitive societies even today will adopt to resolve what is otherwise unfinished at times of death. Did a kinsman die "naturally" or because of someone's ill will? Was that ill will conscious or unintended? Was the malicious feeling transmitted through magic or sorcery, through legitimate means or through foul? The dead person's soul, like the questions over why someone died, will not rest until the last word is spoken. In such a society divination discloses the presence, the source and intent, of the magic, and when the rites are properly performed, the community can lay to rest its grievances; various rites, from the wearing to the scattering of ashes, enable the dead and the living to carry on. In a modern society, of course, the autopsy is separate from the trial, and the trial is separate from the funeral; public speculation and recrimination continue because the last word is seldom spoken and a final inclusive judgment on the meaning of certain actions seldom given. Societal pressure for a final test continues to accumulate precisely because the sense of indebtedness has gone underground. Pressure to settle accounts can eventually shatter the containers of ritual and release hatred and a desire for revenge into everyday social life. *Rambo* and *Death Wish* become serials in a continuing story, when justice is never done.

Translated into more conventional language for a sociologist, my argument simply insists on the difference between questions of truth and of reality; I stand in a sociological tradition opposed to a pragmatism that confuses the two kinds of questions, just as it is opposed to a nihilism that relativizes every social reality and begs the truth question. Individuals with good intentions and good minds are never isolated either from class conflict or from bureaucratic regulation as they seek to arrive at the most appropriate course of action. The majority work under pressure or coercion and make judgments endowed—at the best—with purely "formal" rather than "substantive" rationality. The majority of people do not make big decisions, C. Wright Mills argued; these decisions are made under the pressure of events in settings where bureaucracies pull and conflict tugs—not in fireside chats or strolls through the woods but in internal war carried out in bureaucratic chambers and on the streets. Nonetheless, American society continues to scapegoat individuals who are its victims. That is how a sacrificial complex works, and is a manifestation of the Daedalus complex.

The Secularization of Guilt and Responsibility:
The Eclipse of Sin in Complex Societies

I might summarize these general observations about secularization by quoting Bryan Wilson, the perennial theorist of the secular:

> Religious perceptions and goals, religiously induced sensitivities, religiously-inspired morality, and religious socialization appear to be of no immediate relevance to the operation of the modern social system. . . . Planning, not revelation; rational order, not inspiration; systematic routine, not charismatic or traditional action, are the imperatives . . . of public life. (1982:76–177)

Wilson (1982:173) also reminds us that the achieving of spiritual heights by a religious elite always has the effect of secularizing daily life for ordinary individuals who cannot find in such rarefied religious teaching a rhetoric for the expression of their deepest motives and most fearful impulses. Religious elites make the big spiritual decisions and leave the average individual more than ever confined to the mundane. C. Wright Mills would agree. Under these conditions the churches' traditional rhetoric for sin does seem out of keeping with the surface experience of everyday life for those who have no big decisions to make or big sins to confess. The memory of those sins is not grievous, and their burden is not intolerable, at least not on the surface of social life.

To make spiritual achievements or political and economic decisions the privilege of an elite hardly enlightens or liberates the individual who is confined by bureaucratic routines or the highly limited responsibilities of the laity. Managers and professionals, who govern the requirements of a specialized ordering of work, may enjoy "privileged communication" or "sacred" relationships with their clients. But professionals and bureaucracies offer little opportunity or scope for individuals to confess what is in their hearts or to lay hold of their salvation in the world of work and politics. Certainly secularization has reduced religion's authority to define the expression of human motives in specific actions.

More "primitive" societies do enact, in symbolic form, irrational impulses of self-hatred, envy, rebellion, and murder (cf. Turner 1969). The "enemy" or "victim" to be overcome or sacrificed may be anyone who threatens the individual's essential supplies of food, protection, self-esteem, and love. More complex societies, however, often provide a more muted expression of murderous impulses. Magical thinking and the impulse to eliminate all competition from one's life do not disappear, however, even when the modern adult learns to speak rationally or appears to take responsibility for his or her own life. Witness also the public fascination with journeys to outer space and with video games that feature a haunted, pursued creature in a labyrinth. That labyrinth, whether it is a modern maze or the original creation of Daedalus, is still a fitting symbol of the unconscious and its tortuous control of our lives. In the absence of adequate solemnizations, however, individuals find their own personal pathway and absolve themselves of their own guilt. The lack of corporate absolution and a common pathway leaves the individual with an unprecedented burden of responsibility without either a promise of fulfillment and release or a corporate yardstick by which to measure self-deception. Even the society's "offscourings," its unemployed, its failures, and its uncounted citizens too obscure to be enumerated in the census, are eliminated without ceremony. In limbo, they become sources of possible pollution and disturbance and raise demands for societal purity. The Daedalus complex has therefore only been protracted and attenuated, submerged and sublimated. It may return with a new demand for purity and satisfaction, with calls for fresh victims or a final settling of accounts.

In the first chapter I introduced the Daedalus myth in order to show how a sacrificial system works. I am using the notion of the Daedalus complex in this book as a metaphor to suggest that every system operates on the basis of sacrifice. Whether those sacrifices are more or less obvious, focused on specific victims, and ritualized depends on the type of society. The system "works" at all because of latent emotional residues of childhood, residues that leave the adult with a sense of unpaid debts and an obligation to pay them—with the awareness that he or she has been living at the expense of others. Rituals have been one means by which any society evokes that sense of obligation, enables individuals to discharge their debts to the living and the dead, and either cancels that debt or recycles it to a later generation. Modern societies have been drawing on these psychological residues of childhood and have now reached the point of diminishing returns. Many individuals, for instance, have been increasingly unwilling to make sacrifices of time and energy, of the heart or the intellect. Nonetheless, modern societies have not been able to satisfy unconscious desires for a satisfaction of debts—the desire of individuals to settle accounts, to make their last payment on their debt to society, or to receive what they believe are their entitlements. Pressures for such a settlement of accounts explain masochistic tendencies that are expressed in apocalypticism, demands for rebirth, and millennial strivings, as well as in quieter forms of despair that are suddenly politicized.

3

A Brief Typology
of
Psychological Indebtedness

———➤✠◄———

There are many kinds of psychological indebtedness; some, for instance, to the sources of life, and others to a social world whose boundaries ward off the threat and fear of death. This is an inquiry into the general sense of indebtedness that one either owes a "debt to society" or is entitled to various honors and satisfactions. The feeling that one has yet to pay one's debt to the community or the society is expressed in a mild or even at times extreme feeling of dread of a day of reckoning. Conversely, the feeling that one is entitled to certain satisfactions or to a recognition that one has not yet received is expressed in a chronic *despair* at ever receiving one's due. Indeed, such despair may at times become quite acute. When it does, there may well be a demand for a day of reckoning.

Religion, of course, has been a major custodian of social hopes and fears and has been able to stimulate, sustain, and periodically satisfy both dread and despair. In a secular society one may have to look elsewhere, for example, to popular culture, mass entertainment, and the private preoccupations of individual citizens, to tap the despair and the dread that may persist without being the subject of collective religious enthusiasm or ritual. The demand for a day of reckoning is therefore easier to assess in a society where religion is pervasive, popular, and well institutionalized. Under such conditions, the suffering of individuals is easily publicized and acted out in dramatic form—revivals calling for fire from heaven, preaching from more elegant pulpits with more abstract symbols of a day of judgment, and elaborate statements by ecclesiastical committees that calculate the balance between society's debts to the individual and the individual's debts to the larger society. In a society where days of reckoning are imagined in terms of a nuclear apocalypse, of an invasion by aliens from space, or of the demonic revenge of estranged adolescents, the screen and the paperback become the more visible pulpits for evoking dread, not to mention the warnings of pop singers that "a hard rain's a-gonna fall."

Debt to the Source of Life

The first type of debt is owed, I suggest, to *charisma*. Now "charisma" is a term with many meanings in sociological literature; its strict construction differs considerably from the more popular usage of journalists who look (often in vain) for charisma in candidates for presidential office. By charisma I wish to convey any person or institution that claims to offer (and is attributed with being able to control) the sources of life. Parents have charisma in the eyes of their children, who see them as beings somewhat larger than life precisely because the parents possess the secret of the child's origin, can sustain or destroy the child, and can be summoned but neither possessed nor controlled. Those who have died in war or in a disaster often acquire a certain charisma, as if they died so that the survivors could live. The feeling that one owes one's life to one's parents or to those whom one has survived can leave a residue of feelings of obligation that sometimes only death itself can assuage. The sense that one owes one's life to one's parents can be expressed in a desire to die for the mother-or father-land. In the same fashion, survivors make their lives a

memorial to those who died in their stead and offer sacrifices of the heart and soul. Some die of remorse and
grief. Others offer themselves as a living sacrifice and
live a life of dying-to-please. If they live in dread of being called to account and of being made to offer a final
sacrifice, it is a fear that they wish to have; it is the price
of keeping alive the hope for access to the sources of
life, of special favor, and of rescue.

Those who hunger and thirst for charismatic sources
of life and renewal can also encounter despair along the
way. The child who waits for the parent's return, like
the devotee who longs for the blessed vision, often de-
spairs of living to see the day or moment of "salvation."
I speak of salvation in a nontechnical sense, as being a
state of mind in which one feels whole and fully alive.
Often the longing for access to charisma is expressed as
a desire to be seen by the parent or savior, a passive
longing rather than the more active desire for a vision.
In this passive sense the desire for the presence of charisma is a hunger for recognition, as if in being saved the
individual will be given the same gift of life as the charismatic is thought to possess. For the redeemer to "lift
up the light of the countenance upon" the believer ac-
complishes the same infusion of life-giving spirit as the
believer's own vision of the savior.

In pursuit of secular sources of charisma, individuals
can search for a glimpse of celebrities, entertainers, candidates for office, and other dignitaries; they also can
seek more routine sources of recognition from institutions that, after considerable probing and testing, offer
tokens of high regard, such as licenses, degrees, and
other certificates of recognition. The point is that charisma can come from sacred and secular sources, be
sought actively or passively, and still leave a residual
despair that the individual will never succeed in gain-
ing access to charisma or to the long-sought-after
recognition.

In modern societies officials and politicians still acquire charisma by preserving the life and preventing the premature and unnatural death of the environment, of communities, and of the people themselves. For instance, in the United States, politicians hungry for legitimacy declare "wars" on poverty, drugs, or cancer. The social contract still holds officialdom per se responsible for life and death; bad deaths, like the casualties of the Vietnam War, can cast a long shadow on the legitimacy of a regime and even of the state itself. Nonetheless, there is little impulse to try leaders *personally* for war crimes in the United States, and even less impulse to hold them personally responsible for the deaths of infants whose families are deprived of nutritional and medical support. In modern societies official guilt has become largely impersonal. Dissent places blame on the leaders of the people as officeholders rather than as individuals—certainly not on the people themselves. Regularly scheduled elections and the occasional use of the right to recall public officials substitute in the United States for rituals of scapegoating. Regardless of the destruction caused by drought or by war, by mismanaged utilities and transportation, this country seldom holds officials personally responsible or turns grief and rage into revolutionary dissent.

In many contemporary societies other than the United States, however, social ills and premature deaths are still experienced as personal tragedies by both leaders and people. In some Central American societies, earthquakes in the 1970s and 1980s may have had profound political consequences (cf. Levine 1986). In South Korea the premature, violent death of a student in police custody has led to political demonstrations, riots, and some fatalities among both police and demonstrators. The future of the regime was not only precarious; the political system itself was confronted with such opposition that a major change from authoritarian to democratic institutions might well have developed. Bad deaths can shake the social system even in contemporary societies that embody residues of the traditional social contract. When both leaders and people share the same dread of unfulfilled obligations and of unpaid debts to the sources of life and death, tragedy can have revolutionary implications.

Contrast the implicit social contract in the United States. An interview with the current president of Manville, an asbestos vendor, makes it clear how limited is the liability of American elites (*New York Times,* Oct. 9, 1988:III, 1). The company has been allowed now by the Supreme Court to go back to business as a public trust; 80 percent of its stock and 20 percent of its annual profits will go to pay its victims, many of whom, of course, have already died from poisoning by asbestos. The company fought hard against the claims brought by those whose lives have been damaged or lost by exposure to asbestos; it gave no quarter. According to Manville's president, the company was voted the "least admired" of all American businesses in a recent survey by *Fortune,* but the president claimed that the company had risen since then to five places from the bottom. The new president apparently sees his job as restoring pride in the company, getting the company moving again, and bringing its productive efforts to bear on its mission, that is, to compensate those damaged or killed by its products. The tone of the interview is upbeat, full of imagery about making the "tough calls," getting "a move on," and getting the "pride" back. The new president frankly acknowledges the pain he underwent as a result of the corporation's experience: the humiliation of having his American Express card refused when the company went bankrupt, the days away from his family, and the need for restoring corporate self-respect by earning public approval. He "prays for" and "empathizes with" the victims, whom he thinks about daily. It is time, however, to think about the future. The president spoke about being "world class" in the future and about setting, in the present, "higher standards than everybody else" to redeem the company's name from taint. The image he seemed to prefer for this rebirth was that of the phoenix rising from its ashes. It was the company that had to be rejuvenated, not the individuals who had died or sickened. Its past was filled with "mistakes" and "problems," not with evil or wrongdoing. As for moral judgments, the company was simply being held responsible for social standards that had become less permissive in recent years than they were during the 1930s and 1940s, when the "problems" and "mistakes" occurred. That was in the past. The company is now being judged by the values of a society that has changed, and the company will change along with it. Now "the subject is how do you build a company that can create the value that can pay our bills." The ones who made the "mistakes" are gone. The injuries have been suffered. No one can reverse the clock. There is no use in self-punishment; "the next job is to be a normal company." That means contributing jobs to the economy and "value for our shareholders." When it comes to standards and moral judgments, then, Manville simply is a reflection of the larger society. When it comes to jobs, products, and "value" (whatever that is), Manville is going to be world class. There is great pride here in what a company can do; nothing is said about being morally self-determining or responsible. If higher than ordinary standards are needed for the company to regain its public standing, that is because of what the president referred to as "the Manville mistake." There are a number of questions about ethics that the president of Manville is loath to raise; I will leave it to the ethicists to point them out. What concerns me is the apparent absence of dread—dread of judgment for having blighted the lives of thousands and for having caused the premature death of more that still remain to be counted. Where is the corporate sense of indebtedness to the sources of life? Where is the sense of sin beyond the awareness of a taint to the company name?

In more "primitive" societies, the death of someone from unnatural causes was a source of evil to the community; the dead might well seek compensation of a sort that no one would be willing to pay. Certainly they might seek compensation that a company like Manville would be unwilling to pay, even if it becomes "world class." The notion of an eye for an eye may be primitive, but it has the virtue of expressing exactly what both the living victims and the dead might have in mind. A better compensation might be sought by the living whose lives have been made painful, bleak, and full of suffering. They too might seek something commensurate: more in the way of an eye for an eye than 20 percent of the profits. We know that money cannot adequately pay for blighted and lost lives; there is nothing commensurate to such losses in a society based on money as the primary medium of exchange. My question, however, is not about the ethics of such payments; it is about the sense of dread that a community—or a company—might be expected to have under these conditions: dread before a day of final accounting.

Dread is subjective—the sense of unfulfilled obligation. What makes dread personal is the sense that one is liable oneself for this unsatisfied debt. A more corporate sense of dread underlies the awareness that a community or a nation, an organization or an institution, owes a debt that will be most painful or even impossible to discharge, the sense notably missing in the talk of the current Manville president. When corporate dread finds a willing victim, one who is glad to satisfy the collective debt with personal sacrifice, the community has found the ideal scapegoat—a troublemaker, someone infectious, who can be made willingly to pay the price. The sense of an unsatisfied obligation, of a debt that remains to be paid, of a payment that will be exacted somehow of someone, is the mark of the sense of dread, and its remedies require more than the payment of stock dividends as compensation.

Where has the sense of dread gone in modern societies? There is in many myths a sense that the gods are owed something; they will exact their payment at a time of their own choosing, and it may not be the one preferred by the priests in charge of the more ritualized payment of debts at the local sanctuary. In the Daedalus myth, King Minos's crime of having kept something of Poseidon's for himself underlies the eventual collapse of Minos's empire. Poseidon demanded unreserved sacrifice, gifts commensurate with his divinity, with nothing held back. It was a debt that only the god could have paid, and in providing the white bull for sacrifice he did provide the means of payment. Minos's next payment therefore was to be far more painful, its suffering more widespread, its calamity more disastrous than ritualized sacrifice, because his first offering was not pure or wholehearted. Daedalus thus created a labyrinth for him, at the heart of which was a symbol of the king's greed: a Minotaur who ravishes the queen and devours the youth of Athens.

There is nothing on this order in the public statements of the Manville president. The lives lost, the health never regained, the hopes disappointed—these are not repaid by the notion of a corporation rising like a phoenix from its ashes. No phoenix can take flight on the wings of the annual report of a corporation. Like Minos, Manville withheld and delayed payments. Like Minos, Manville aspires to being world class. The aspirations of the king were defeated by his holding back the payment to Poseidon; hence the sense of dread that an unfulfilled obligation would yet have to be paid at terrible expense. I see no comparable sense of a debt to past and future

generations and to the survivors of the present one in the
Manville president's utterances. Certainly there is no anticipation of a final accounting on a day of divine judgment, when all such bills fall due and payable; neither is
there a dread of a public shaming ritual. The president
argued:

> What is Manville? Are you talking about punishing the indi-
> viduals or are you talking about taking the corporate char-
> ter and nailing it to the wall and whipping it? Whom do you
> want to punish? Do you want to go back and find anybody
> who's still alive who made mistakes in the 30s and 40s? If
> you do, that's criminal law. We're talking about civil proce-
> dures here. We're talking about economic issues. (*New
> York Times,* Oct. 9, 1988:III, 1)

The language of "procedures" and "issues" begs the
question of morality and wrongdoing, of corporate responsibility and guilt, that the interviewer, along with
ethicists and theologians, wanted to raise. My question is
where the sense of an unpaid obligation has gone. Surely
the debt to the living and the dead is more than an obligation to pay court-determined dividends to the victims
of the corporation.

The settlement itself suggests that there is a debt that
the corporation has to pay with its life. The court has
ruled that "as much as" 80 percent of the stock and 20
percent of the profits must go to the victims and their
families. It is as if a corporation that has been too greedy
has been swallowed up by its victims. There is an eye-for-
an-eye aspect to this judgment. The life that the corporation lives is now the life of its former victims. Dead to its
old self, the corporation now lives in the body, so to
speak, of its former victims. It is they who own the lion's
share of the stock. The corporation's all-consuming passion for profits and market share devoured its workers;
now its victims have consumed the corporation and will
consume much of its profits in the future. In the Pac-Man

game of corporate acquisitions, this is all that remains of an eye for an eye, stock ownership for lost and blighted lives. Where, then, is the dreadful recognition of the debt, not only to greed but also to the dead and maimed, that has to be paid in the currency of modern societies, that is, in dividends and stocks?

What is missing from the talk of "economic issues" and "civil procedures" is any sense of an unpaid and unpayable debt, that is, dread itself. Psychoanalysts have no hesitation in identifying greed, an insatiable, all-consuming hunger, as the dominant human motive. Residues of the early organism's attempt to guarantee its life by swallowing everything in its path persist in the adult as a sin stemming from humanity's infinite, animal-like origins. One of those residues is exactly the awareness that there is an appetite that has not been assuaged. That is why I insist that desire, compounded with fear, underlies dread.

Under the conditions of repression, of course, this awareness of desire is sublimated into a sense of unfulfilled obligation: a payment that has yet to be made. That is why the term "satisfaction" is used to designate the fulfillment of a debt as well as the relief of an appetite. There is also a sacrificial sense in which "satisfaction" refers to the offering of the worshiper to the god: another debt that is difficult to pay in full. That antique usage survives in liturgical language, as in the "satisfaction" for sin offered by the Son of God on the cross. The debt is to a God who is literally never satisfied; it is one debt that can never be paid in full. This is why this sin is original.

Where, then, in public statement, or in public policy, for that matter, is there recognition of the destructive effects of the most common, garden-variety source of evil, ordinary greed? In the rites of traditional societies there is more dramatic recognition of the danger of greed in the hearts of the ruler. In rites of passage into high office the chief or the king is reminded of how much he owes to the ordinary members of the community and is warned against forgetting his debt to them. Minos's later destructiveness stems from his holding back a part of himself rather than giving himself entirely to the office; that is why he uses the office for personal gain.

The entire Daedalus myth constitutes a cautionary tale against self-aggrandizing tendencies in both the old and the young. Daedalus himself is moved by envy to destroy his brilliant young nephew; Icarus rises too high, too soon, and in failing to follow his father's instructions destroys himself. His disastrous end signifies the danger of an incomplete transition: a failed rite of passage. The myth may well have accompanied rites of passage from youth into adulthood, from everyday life into early mysteries, or from the rank of novice to that of craftsman. The point is that the myth, and the accompanying rites, made no secret of the destructive potential of greed. In modern societies greed has become the object of psychoanalysis, the subject of theater and movie dramatizations and of journalistic commentary. Still, in corporate discourse, greed has been relegated to the margins of a text devoted to procedures and issues, questions of fact and questions of law, expert opinion and theories of public liability.

What is suppressed in the language of such formal organizations as the corporation or the court is quite volubly expressed—still in the public sphere—by a continuous series of exposés: greed in corporate America, greed in the professions, greed in the family. The chronicles of destruction at the hands of corporations mindless of their responsibility to the public continue unabated. The names Silkwood, Love Canal, Buffalo Creek, Three Mile Island, Morton Thiokol, A. H. Robins, G. D. Searle, and the like have become a lectionary of greed and destruction. The demand for more information on the seduction of children by parents, of

patients by doctors and therapists, of smokers by to-
bacco companies, of stockholders by inside traders,
seems as insatiable as the hunger that underlies greed
itself. Despite the insistence of some that Americans
have lost their tongue on the subject of corporate and
collective responsibility, publishing houses still have to
struggle to keep up with the demand for more revela-
tions and more judgments.

These highly publicized commentaries, however, do
not seem to inspire a dread of judgment or a collective
sense of sin. The sense of some unfulfilled and unfillable
obligation, owed by those most responsible for the destruction of lives and of the environment, seems relatively missing even amid the calls for judicial penalties,
compensation to victims, and more stringent legislation.
There seems to be no reckoning that cannot be ac-
counted for in the usual way by the usual procedure.
What has happened to the dread of such an awesome
debt? Is dread simply excluded from public awareness
by the formal language of the academy or the court? Has
that awareness been successfully suppressed? Has the
awareness of a dreadful debt been displaced to other
areas of social life, where it is trivialized, exaggerated,
or disguised beyond recognition? Or has the awareness
of such a hopeless obligation been transformed successfully into a series of lesser debts, like the debt to stockholders and victims, payable in small amounts over a
number of decades, as in the case of Manville? Finally,
does the answer to these questions depend on whether
we are talking about personal or corporate obligation,
impersonal and generic or quite concrete and specific
debts?

Debt to Restore the World

In the rather abstract terms of the president of Manville, the task of the corporation is to create "value," a

fiscal surplus that can be used to pay compensation in the form of dividends to the victims-turned-stockholders. In a society whose forms of compensation are more highly ritualized, the task would be to restore the energies that had been drained—the lives consumed by the greed of the institution. Both modern and traditional societies recognize the need to restore a created order, a world of people and things, that has been depleted and blighted. In some traditional societies, however, annual rites of restoration deliberately sought to guarantee the recreation of the world by a massive outpouring of gifts. Many of these gifts were votive offerings: symbols of the person to be healed or of a limb to be restored or replaced. Entire communities swept their altars clean of the debris of old offerings in order to make room for the new wave of gifts to be consumed in sacrificial fires on a high place (Burkert 1985). In that consuming flame would be restored the life that had been drained from the world in the year immediately past. It is as if one could cure the ill effects of consuming passions by making gifts to a consuming force such as fire and water. In those gifts of life, life itself would be renewed and restored. There was indeed a frank recognition that something must be sacrificed if the world, consumed by greed, was to have new vitality.

Not only the annual votive offerings of traditional societies made this equation between new life and payment of the debt incurred by consumption. To restore the energies of a society it is always necessary for a new generation to replace the old. The vitality of an aging order is only renewed by making places for the next age group to take the positions of adulthood. In these traditional rites of passage, however, the same equation of a life sacrificed for a life spent, so to speak, called for painful and rigorous trials of the young. What was being sacrificed were the all-consuming passions that could destroy the very society that the young were being called upon to save and preserve.

The Daedalus myth makes it clear that Icarus, inattentive to his father's work and instructions, was thus distracted from the rite of passage in which the father carefully coated the boy's body with wax and covered it with feathers like a young male initiate among the Australian aborigines. If the young male initiate is to inherit patriarchal authority, it is necessary that he first be willing to observe the limits placed on his career by his elders. The Phaeton myth also tells the story of youthful greed and aggression. Such careers threaten to consume the entire natural and social order with fire and must be extinguished before it is too late. Better the sacrificial flames than the thunderbolts of Zeus. One must sacrifice the will to live at others' expense in order to avoid paying the terrible tribute to death itself.

I question whether this traditional sense of collective and personal obligation to renew the creation and the social order enters into the discourse of the modern corporation or the court; rather, such awareness has been suppressed entirely, or has at the very least been displaced to the counterculture or into entertainment. Perhaps it has been reduced to something specific and concrete, for example, dividends or rates of corporate growth. The Manville president refers to creating "value," but his level of abstraction is fairly high and his specific reference at best obscure.

Elites in a complex society can avoid recognizing their debts to the natural or social order precisely by stating their obligations in the abstract, as in the use of the terms "justice" and "compensation." The relevance of these terms to a world that has been depleted or drained of its vitality remains obscure, as though the details of the damages done were somewhat beneath the viewpoint of those making "the tough calls" or the corporate policies. As Freud reminded us some time ago, there is an element of the grandiose in this apparent obliviousness to the minutiae of life and to the damage done to the world by one's greedy, destructive motives. There is an element of noblesse oblige in the choice to enunciate values in the abstract without spelling out what precisely is meant in concrete situations. The long distance between the notion of "value" and the very detailed and human litany of sickness and death to specific individuals is one measure of the noblesse oblige of policymakers, lawyers, corporation executives, and ideologues in the social sciences. It is like the noblesse oblige of those who revised the painful litany of the *Book of Common Prayer,* expunging references to specific ills and enunciating appeals for the "common good." Somehow that phrase does not evoke the same awareness of a social world desperate for healing and renewal that was conveyed by the more medieval references in the litany, for example, to plague, famine, and sudden death. The abstractions of a modern society are thus the expressions of a modern noblesse oblige that prefers to keep its obligations minimal and unspecified.

It would be difficult, if not impossible, to describe adequately the various remedies with which modern societies are now trying to restore a world that has been damaged through one form of greed or another. Certainly some of the debts are discharged in quite specific ways—in kind rather than in cash. Alternate forms of punishment allow a variety of services to the community to take the place of discharging a "debt" to society behind bars. In a society whose exchanges are largely in cash, however, sanctions on corporations and individuals alike are largely monetary. Of course, there are exceptions and perhaps even countertrends. Some corporations that engage in activities destructive of the environment now seek specific ways of restoring the natural order; one utility has been recently reported as planning to plant a forest in Guatemala in order to counterbalance its own emissions of carbon dioxide, a specific remedy exactly proportioned to its own manner of damaging the environment. In any event, in a society that relies more on rationalized than on ritualized methods of discharging debt, the method of payment will be rational, whether or not it is generic, as in the use of money, or quite specific, as in alternative forms of community service or conservation.

In many ways modern societies make more effective use of the passions and anguish associated with the destruction and blighting of human life, perhaps more effective use than traditional societies that relied almost entirely on repetitive and protracted ritual. The Protestant Reformation, for instance, succeeded in attacking the rites performed for the dead; the practice of indulgences was particularly offensive to the Reformers. Instead of wasting devotion, time, money, heartache, and piety on the dead, the Reformation made a virtue of the careful expenditure of money, love, and trust on the serious business of living. Instead of keeping the perennial appointments with the dead, the Protestants enshrined the keeping of one's temporal appointments. Instead of wasting resources on debts to the past, Reformed religion encouraged the careful husbandry of resources in the present for the future. Devotion to the dead is a waste of time; such devotion laments the loss of time and keeps the past alive by enshrining it as a living memory and as the communion of the saints. The Protestant Reformation turned the stewardship of time into a virtue and substituted the payment of debts over time for the payment of sacred obligations to the departed. The communion of the saints made way for the communion of the living congregation, whose industry was an attempt to make up for lost time.

Debt to the Departed

Of course, there have been earlier contests between the demands of the living and the dead. Burkert (1985) tells us that the heroes of the polis were in competition with the honors paid to the dead of noble families in ancient Greece; Western cities have had to absorb the devotion encapsulated in the family and expended on ancestors in order to transform the obligations of kinship into those of citizenship. The effectiveness of Western societies in absorbing this surplus of devotion in the form of more rational and routine obligations to work and politics is a centerpiece of Weberian scholarship.

It takes more than work and politics, however, to satisfy the sense of obligation to the dead. Danforth's (1982) recent study of funeral laments in rural Greece makes the same point that Malinowski and later anthropologists have been making for years: that feelings for the dead are so intense and ambivalent that they require expensive and complex funeral rites. In Greece still the dead are offered food and gifts, partly as a reaction against the greedier emotions of the survivors, elated as they may be at the prospect of inheritance, partly as a way of satisfying the longing of the family to continue to provide for someone they have cared for over the years. Lifton's work with the survivors of death and disaster points out how important it is for the living to reenact death scenes by coming to the rescue of those in danger, by providing care for the hungry and needy, and by restoring life wherever it is threatened. This surplus of desire to save the dead may stem from a desire to pay back those who have injured one; it may stem from a desire to return love for love received. The unconscious law of an eye for an eye is expressed in a variety of ritualized payments, many of them quite specific, as in the offering of food for the dead, or surrendering one's most precious possession. Indeed, the surplus of such funerary devotion has enriched many sanctuaries and shrines. They became sources of treasure that warlords and zealots in antiquity found irresistible, as have more recent monarchs and führers. The more routine and rational appropriation of these offerings, in work and industry, in politics and nation building, rather than through the depredations of religious and military charismatics, is—in the Weberian analysis—the central achievement of the West. The question is whether the Westerner finds the system's arrangements *satisfying,* regardless of how *effective* they may be in ensuring that devotion is now lavished upon the living rather than the dead.

It is easier for a modern corporation to cut its losses than for an individual to do so, when those losses are as personal and painful as grief and bereavement suggest. To "declare Chapter 11" gives a corporation time to fend off its creditors; it is a declaration of moratorium on indebtedness to the dead and to their survivors who might, along with living victims, wish to make claims against the company. It is somewhat more difficult for a modern nation to declare Chapter 11 to protect itself from the claims of the survivors, say, of the Vietnam War. Those debts are still being paid. Still, it is far easier for a nation and for a corporation to "put paid" to their debts to the past than for an individual to cut his or her losses.

Even the phrase "cutting your losses" is painfully pointed, like the sting of death itself. The image of cutting suggests the anger and the anguish that survivors feel—anger at the loss and frustration imposed by death, and at the helplessness and remorse experienced by the living when confronted with the dead, not to mention the residues of anger toward the deceased for insults and injuries, real and imaginary, sustained over a lifetime by the survivors. To cut your losses suggests, like biting the hand that feeds you, the most profound and ambivalent emotions of hate and love. It is this ambivalence that gives death its "sting." Some tribes rend garments; others have men brandish swords and spears. The Greeks gave expression to these passions in long, agonized laments but also in games and contests after the funeral itself was over. In those contests were fought out the rival claims of the living and the dead for love and devotion, for gifts and for the sacrifice of time and attention.

The games were ritualized ways of adjudicating the claims of the dead on the living, which now are decided by courts in long, agonizing judicial contests. No doubt these legal battles, expensive as they are in time and money, are effective in absorbing some of the surplus devotion toward the deceased not taken up in funeral rites. They remove some of the sting from death. No doubt also the court system resolves enough of the contest between the living and the dead to enable corporations to go back to work in the present with minimal obligations to the deceased.

Nonetheless, for the individuals concerned these obligations constitute the unsatisfied and unconsummated desires of the living to pay the dead some measure of their devotion. This unpaid residue of obligation may be experienced as a sense of dread: a sinful apprehension of a more complete reckoning and calling to account. Individuals may remain spooked even in traditional societies long after their equivalent of All Hallows Eve; rituals do not always work equally well for everyone. In the same way, how many individuals in modern societies remain haunted by a sense of their indebtedness to previous generations in ways that cannot be paid either in legal settlements or in the careful accounting and stewardship of time and money still sanctioned by the Reformed religious traditions?

It would be a mistake, of course, to portray modern societies entirely in terms of court routines and the procedures for paying compensations to the living on behalf of the dead and dying. Nonetheless, I believe that a secularized underworld exists even in these contemporary societies, a residual form of the limbo that in antiquity constituted the world of departed spirits. Funerary practices still found in Greece—gathering the remains, putting them in boxes, endowing the underground world with a life of its own, and so forth—resemble in some ways the rites that visitors to a much earlier Hellenistic underworld may have participated in (Danforth 1982). In the United States the Mormons have become genealogical virtuosos, the custodians of records of the dead in many Western societies from all religious or secular backgrounds. As the extraordinary growth of the Mormons in this country and elsewhere suggests, there is a residue of unsatisfied devotion remaining to be tapped, a vast, latent desire to fulfill obligations to the past.

Obligation to Purify Society

The collective disregard of sin in modern societies can be illustrated by examining the ways traditional communities and societies purified themselves of evils. In Jerusalem in the first century, for instance, the evils of the society were purged daily; two lambs were consumed in the sacrificial fires on each day, much to the astonishment of the Hellenistic-Roman world at the time (Burkert 1985), itself no stranger to collective rites of purification. Indeed, there was an important commerce that supported these rites; it brought produce and wealth from the country to the city, enriched the Temple and its priesthood, and supported craftsmen of the city. The resulting economic benefits trickled slowly back to the countryside. A severe depression followed the destruction of the Temple in the civil war of 66–70 c.e. In other words, the sacrifices of collective purification were fundamental to the politics and the economy as well as to the sacred institutions of Palestinian society.

No less systematic are the corporate "evils" of sexism and racism in the contemporary United States. These are expunged, however, by the slow and careful working of programs of equal opportunity or affirmative action, collective bargaining, and litigation. The sacrifices are no less costly than those in traditional societies, perhaps, but the rites are those of the bureaucracy and the court rather than of the temple. In both societies elites administer these sacrifices according to law (sacred or secular). The obligation to sacrifice falls disproportionately on those of higher status—the "noblesse" in each case "oblige." The legitimacy of elites in both modern and traditional societies involves the purification of the body politic and its corporate sins. Both sacrificial systems have widespread ramifications in the political and economic life of the society. The traditional system involves repetitive, discrete, ceremonial acts; the modern system is linear, continuous, and consists of administrative actions. The former prescribes how much is enough; the latter negotiates the question of sufficiency. In modern societies, the open-ended discussion of how much is enough keeps open the quest for purity. It absorbs and utilizes the desire for a social world, pure, spotless, and purged of impurities, without satisfying it.

Not all the techniques for corporate purification are of this generic nature. (By "generic" I refer to the interchangeability of lambs and bulls of comparable perfection or to the abstract notion of racism or sexism by which discrete instances of sin are made comparable.) Some of these corporate techniques make use of sacrificial victims that are one of a kind. As was mentioned in the introduction, some Mediterranean communities in Greece of the last millennium B.C.E. selected a criminal for sacrificial purposes and pushed him into the sea, perhaps equipping him with makeshift wings fabricated for the occasion. It was customary in many cities of antiquity to select a criminal on annual occasions to be scapegoated; the procedures often involved marching the victim through the streets, mock respect and public humiliation, and dressing the victim in rich vestments before leading him (or possibly her) to the boundaries of the city to be expelled or stoned to death. As in modern societies, the victims were usually the more vulnerable members of the community and distinguished by characteristics that made them repugnant: weakness, the taint of imperfection, impurity, disease, or other forms of wretchedness.

Many of the victims of Nazi Germany were described as filth or vermin regardless of their relatively high levels of education and achievement. It is significant that the first victims were visibly tainted by physical or mental impairments. The selection of scapegoats in traditional and modern societies is similar, therefore, in some respects: It includes the same attention to stigma of various sorts; the same attempt at purification through eliminating sources of trouble, disorder, or impurity in the population; the same attempt to mobilize public opinion against the scapegoat; and the same use of what Girard (1987) calls the ritual machinery of scapegoating. That machinery in modern societies is provided by the state, supported by local organizations, informers, and the police. In traditional societies the machinery also made use of secrecy but required public acclamation and utilized the open spaces of the community. In both instances scapegoating mobilized the public desire for a purified body politic and satisfied it with the obligatory death of some victim chosen for his or her specific characteristics, imperfections, stigmas, or particular offense.

In traditional societies the debt to society, that is, the obligation to allow the community to purify itself at the expense of a victim, was paid in rites that inspired considerable excitement and fear (i.e., dread). In modern societies, however, the bureaucratic procedures that are used to purify the system—the machinery of the state, its courts and presses, police and cooperating organizations—work continuously and smoothly without inspiring much awe. When the gavel comes down, cases are closed, but there is no moment of dread as the victim is led off to the boundaries of the society or the corporation assents to the settlement. The procedures are more effective in identifying the ones to be punished than in satisfying the desire for purification.

Whether the scapegoating involves generic or specific techniques, however, the process of scapegoating in modern societies fails to inspire the awe or dread that accompanies the sacrifice of victims in antiquity. There is a certain obviousness to the machinery of the state in modern societies; its very ordinariness and routine suggested to Hannah Arendt the notion of "the banality of evil," as she put it.

Dread used to attend the sacrifice of a particular criminal, a Jonah, a diseased individual during a time of plague, a troublemaker during a period of disorder, an elderly person during drought or famine when supplies were running terribly short and the destruction of the entire society seemed possible. Under these conditions the process of selection must be made to seem inevitable, beyond second guessing, ultimately right, in order to satisfy a sacred obligation to an otherwise destructive god. To avert such wrath is indeed a dreadful responsibility.

Contrast with such rites the machinery of the modern state. As I have noted, Girard (1987) suggests that scapegoating becomes less satisfying the more the "ritual machinery" is visible, obvious, and clearly mechanical. If the victim does not cooperate but protests his or her innocence, the machinery grinds even more audibly, as in the case of political trials in the West or in the routine course of litigation in civil as well as criminal suits in the United States. The courts may be very effective in finding citizens who are to be punished for certain crimes, but the process leaves unsatisfied the public demand for purifying the community of its evils. The names Howard Beach and Bernard Goetz call up events that illustrate this chronic dissatisfaction with the outcome of judicial scapegoating, as do the names "the Chicago Seven" and "the Catonsville Nine." Scapegoating continues in the aftermath of litigation as the public turns to its officials, the press, and television, or to sociologists, liberals, immigrants, and experts, in order to find suitable targets of the demand for purity. Unable to satisfy the demand for purity, modern societies may revert to the more dramatic techniques of Nazi Germany or Cambodia. Recourse to these extreme measures is more likely in a society that inspires little dread and fails at the same time to be effective in purifying itself of poverty, disease, criminals, and the more secret forms of domestic violence. The people's sense of sin, of being tainted and impure, will demand explicit satisfactions.

Added to such corporate afflictions in both traditional and modern societies are the generic ills that plague individuals. It may seem strange to describe personal problems as generic; there does not seem to be anything abstract or general about depression, for instance, when it afflicts one. Nonetheless, the notion of depression as a clinically defined syndrome puts the affliction in the realm of the generic. To do so may satisfy the wishes of practitioners who can then suggest remedies, perhaps forms of therapy in which they themselves happen to specialize. It may also satisfy individuals to find out that they suffer from a relatively well-known ailment; they are not alone with a foreign agent in their soul but rather are still in the realm of the familiar. Jesus, in saying the name of the demon by whom certain sufferers were possessed, may have alleviated this sense of being held captive by an intrusive, powerful, and alien presence, whether it is called Legion or some name with no allusion to the Roman presence. Indeed, there were many "demons" afflicting people in antiquity, and not only in Palestine; the Greeks also knew their names. The popularity of certain legendary figures could be attributed to their ability to expel demons. Solomon was widely celebrated in the Hellenistic world as just such a figure. In the popular *Testament of Solomon* he is reputed to have built the Temple without hands by commanding the demons to carve and place each stone, a feat that may have inspired popular anticipation that a "Son of Solomon" would come who also could expel demons, bind them, make them do his bidding, and thus build a new Temple without manual labor. Like the votive offerings thrown on sacrificial fires by individuals seeking to cure themselves or others of injuries and ailments, the demons were familiar and generic—household names for depression, headache, insomnia, infertility, and a hostile spouse. Exorcisms could be very satisfying to the one possessed; purification brought relief. Nonetheless, exorcism was less effective than satisfying. Demons could—and did—return, and worse ones could take their place. In the meantime, they would invade someone else's house, soul, or herd and cause havoc there. The rites of purification for generic personal ills, like those for corporate evils, were more awe-inspiring and dread-ful than effective.

There are also forms of dread that are specific to each individual and often quite concrete in their manifestations: paralyzed limbs, chronic heaviness about the chest, and all the other ills that we have learned to call psychosomatic. Often these ills are defined in generic terms as syndromes or demonic possessions rather than as signs of such sins as sloth and melancholy. I am now speaking, however, of sin experienced and understood as uniquely personal. In psychoanalytic terms, these are ills that can only be understood by knowing the person's particular history of insults and injuries, both given and received, both real and imaginary. These ills, like sins themselves, now are described in psychoanalytic terms as expressions of desires that the symptoms both express and disguise, fulfill and frustrate. The unconscious sources of dread are thus unconscious crimes for which individuals are suffering punishment.

Conclusion

In this chapter I have focused on four types of obligation: the debt to greed, the debt to a world depleted or destroyed by greed, the debt to the departed, and now the debt to purify the community or society of its ills—a debt to society. Each of the types of obligation is accompanied by a greater sense of sin and dread in traditional as opposed to modern societies. The causes of that diminished sense of sinfulness in a society such as that of the United States require spelling out in terms of sociological and psychological theory.

Our task, however, is to answer the question of why there is any dread in any society, traditional or modern. To understand the nature of personal wishes and fears and how they become translated into social obligation, I will necessarily have to discuss some rudimentary psychoanalytic notions. What, for instance, is the desire that underlies the wish for purity and the fear of contamination? The only pure, homeostatic, undisturbed environment that any individual is likely to occupy is, of course, the womb. On psychoanalytic grounds it is possible to argue that every individual brings to social experience a desire for the purity, stability, and tranquility of the womb, a desire for Nirvana or, as Freud also argued, for death itself. The obligation to purify one's self or one's social environment of disturbing elements is therefore grounded in a wish that is universal, largely unconscious, perennial, and easily disguised and sublimated into duty. The question is whether the resulting obsession with purity involves the individual in community-wide services and national rites or in idiosyncratic and neurotic rituals. The desire for the womb is of course polymorphous, like other infantile wishes, and underlies various forms of a sense of obligation even in modern societies. Whether that desire takes on a form that is perverse or has a "socially redeeming purpose" depends on the structure of the system itself.

Social obligations are fed by unsatisfiable desires, but societies vary in the extent to which they can provide dramatic, however temporary, satisfaction of those desires. Remember that obligations to the dead are derived in large part from a need for the dead, a need for their presence and help, their comfort and rescue. The living turn the tables on the departed by transforming their own desire for rescue into a series of tasks to be performed on behalf of the dead—monuments, memorials, prayer, and other expressions of devotion. There may also be a number of fears that are similarly transformed into obligations to the dead: fears of persecution and retaliation. Underlying these infantile wishes and fears is the wish to return, if not to the womb, at least to the point of one's origin, that magical kingdom in which one's own wishes were others' commands. That wish is intensified, of course, by the desire to return from death itself. The wish for return from death stimulates the regressive wish to get back to the point of one's origin. *There is a surplus of devotion to the dead in any society, therefore, since there are wishes and fears associated with death and life that are intrinsically impossible; one cannot go back to the world of infantile omnipotence any more than one can return from the dead.*

Some societies dramatize obligations to the dead in ways that inspire a sense of awe and dread, while other societies seem less able to draw on this surplus of devotion and turn it into the most serious of social obligations. Indeed, there are polymorphous forms of dread in modern societies: films, detective stories, the occult, and guilty apprehension of apocalyptic devastation when the dead return. However, these multiple expressions of dread drain the surplus of devotion down many channels instead of concentrating them on consummate sacrifices in the political or cultural center. The expressions of dread are, sociologically speaking, perverse as well as polymorphous; as sideshows they do not sustain or add to the supply of obligation at the disposal of the society's dominant institutions and their elites. In anesthetizing itself against the sting of death, any modern society may have lost its capacity to inspire devotion, commitment, and the demand for renewal.

4

An "Outrageous Hypothesis"

————⋇————

Each individual is born with a passion for consumption, an insatiable hunger to fill the self with the contents of the world. That desire, uninformed by the awareness of a sharp distinction between the self and the world, is often experienced as a desire for fusion with the source of life. In religious terms, it is a desire to be at one with the god who is all-in-all, the beginning and the end, the alpha and the omega, the source and the goal of every existence. The desire of the hungry self, along with the desire to be coterminous with the world, yields slowly to the facts of a separate and limited existence. Those who find that separation does not threaten them with death, that the world offers tolerable frustration and reliable nourishment, are likely to accept the reality principle, at least during their waking hours. Others, whose earliest experiences of the world were more painful and frightening, are more likely to demand satisfactions that the world cannot give. In either case, the residues of infancy remain in every adult in the form of a greed that cannot be entirely satisfied.

This debt to desire cannot be paid off or satisfied, no matter what one's pleasures or accomplishments, no matter what one's standing in life. Social life exploits this sense of an unsatisfied longing or debt; the sense of indebtedness becomes a diffuse feeling of obligation and underlies a willingness to take social life seriously. The desire for something "more" becomes experienced as a chronic sense that something more is demanded of the self. That reversal occurs because the unconscious gets things backwards; the self that feels owed comes to feel indebted. The fact of repression makes it difficult for the individual to know just why—or to whom—he or she feels obligated. It is therefore easy for the unconscious to transform every missed opportunity into a payment that has yet to be made—a "return," as it were, on some principal that has not been paid. The payment of such debt makes the business of everyday life serious business indeed. It is *la vie serieuse,* which Durkheim found at the root, the very foundation, of social life.

Ritual Satisfaction of Indebtedness

Not every society, however, allows individuals to reduce this surplus of debt without costly payments or even sacrifice. In societies often described as "traditional," the sense of the surplus of indebtedness is translated into ritual. The primitive potlatch ceremony, in fact, may have been one way of enabling individuals to satisfy such diffuse, unconscious debt. Becker (1976) describes this rite as a collective piling up of goods. The village comes together, as at harvest time, to celebrate its aggregate wealth derived from contributions of food and equipment. Underlying the sense of debt, however, are more destructive emotions like greed. Thus chiefs used to engage in a potlatch ceremony to display their wealth to rival chiefs; the winning chief could afford to offer up and destroy more weapons and canoes, for instance, than the other. I am arguing that an unconscious debt is being satisfied in such rites. Given an all-encompassing desire to consume the world's assets, there can be no such thing as enough. Rites in traditional societies not only provided a dramatic exhibition of the surplus of wealth. They also attempted to satisfy a debt to desire that is inherently beyond satisfaction, because, like sin, it is "original."

Societies that are relatively "modern" have a variety

of techniques other than ritual for absorbing this surplus of debt without creating or maintaining consciousness of sin. Certainly entertainment, games, competitions, and other forms of symbolic rivalry provide satisfaction that is an alternative to ritualized payments of debt. Even more than traditional rites, however, these alternative satisfactions are marginal and fleeting. Unlike those rites, moreover, modern games are not obligatory. Not even the Olympics are required; indeed, the testimony of participants, given in commercials and the media, emphasizes that participation has been based on highly personal motives for individual ends. It is relatively rare, outside of authoritarian societies, to find Olympic athletes claiming a social obligation as their primary motivation. Like pilgrimages or other forms of religious observance, participation in modern games and entertainments is voluntary, optional, and highly geared to the satisfaction of individual ends. Modern societies are therefore more proficient at making use of this surplus of psychological debt than societies that rely more heavily on collective rites. However, modern societies run the danger of exhausting that surplus and entering into a crisis of low motivation and commitment to societal objectives.

This potential crisis of motivation even threatens authoritarian societies that have not until recently enjoyed the benefits of ritual in mobilizing the individual's will to pay. Certainly the introduction of state-sponsored rituals in Soviet Russia reflects a crisis in the ability of that system to generate and sustain adequate commitments in both work and politics (cf. Lane 1981). The bankruptcy of the Stalinist period reminds us, however, that as a totalitarian society the Soviet Union sought to instill a sense of guilt and fear of punishment in the entire population. Speaking of the exportation of Stalinist methods to Cuba under Fidel Castro, Bofill calls guilt the "transcendent weapon that to this day has quashed every effort at reform or political change in the country. The notion was to find and create guilt among the entire population" (*Wall Street Journal,* Feb. 16, 1988:A.15). The same observation underlies the familiar anarchist criticism that original sin was a doctrine designed to make the believer a willing, even sacrificial, source of payments to the body politic.

The dread of being called to account for some unpaid debt is indeed the source of obligation and obedience even in societies in which bureaucrats have replaced the clergy; that was Kafka's point in *The Trial.* I am simply observing that while infancy and childhood provide a surplus of debt that each society seeks to tap for its own purposes, some societies have been more successful than others in stimulating, sustaining, and utilizing this reservoir of commitment and motivation. Modern societies, especially the democracies, have been more effective in utilizing this surplus of debt than were traditional societies, by which I mean societies in which language is the basic institution and that are integrated and divided along lines of kinship. Such societies are segmented into groups according to differences in house or lineage, rather than divided by formal or specialized criteria of competence or class. These ritualized societies, however, were more effective than modern democracies in providing periodic satisfactions of psychological debts in sacrificial rites.

Because sin has become secularized in modern societies, the surplus of psychological indebtedness can be spent in the routine conduct of everyday work and politics—*la vie serieuse.* Given the exhaustion of such residues of psychological debt, modern societies are therefore likely to try to find new methods of generating a sense of indebtedness. Totalitarian societies, as I have noted, have relied on police terror and are now turning to ritual. The democracies may be relying on evangelical and apocalyptic religious movements to generate and sustain fresh reservoirs of motivation and commitment. Hence the topic of sin can be of some interest to sociologists of religion as well as to politicians and bureaucrats interested in guaranteeing safe reserves of *la vie serieuse* in otherwise secularized societies.

It is difficult to know when public discussions of debt and obligation are serious or playful, dreadful or academic. Carroll (1985) observes that Western societies have lost their collective means of talking about guilt, although their literature is obsessed with the topic. Indeed, he rests his claim that guilt is the fundamental problem in Western societies by citing literature from Shakespeare to Nietzsche (1985:4). In resting a case on literary evidence, however, he makes it difficult to know whether these expressions are serious or relevant to dominant social institutions like the courts or modern corporations, or even of some significance to the way a modern society as a whole makes its decisions. It is equally possible that these expressions are playful rather than serious and of no relevance or significance to the larger society. If the market for these or more contemporary literary expressions remains fairly stable, it would make sense to place them in evidence as the expression of psychological debts that are left unpaid by courts and corporations, by the church and the state.

It would be premature, however, to argue that such a sense of indebtedness is still the "vital generative core and virtue of civilization" (Carroll 1985:5). What he assumes is precisely what I take to be problematical. For instance, it is an open question whether dread of a day of accounting has an important social function, or whether the management of such dread is still essential for modern societies if they are to keep people attentive, hard at work, and ready to sacrifice themselves when called upon to do so.

Try looking at it this way. There are many observers of postmodern societies who see the close and playful attention to surfaces, the switching of attention from one channel to another, and the eclectic, shifting popular tastes in food and styles of leadership as evidence that social life is no longer serious. The question, as Todd Gitlin (*New York Times Book Review,* Nov. 6, 1988:1ff.) reminds us, is whether this postmodern preoccupation with the superficial and the changing is a defense against painful and disturbing feelings for which social institutions no longer provide an outlet. Have people changed as a result of the formation of capitalist social classes, the advances of modern science, and the mass media themselves? Is there less dread for modern societies to express and to channel, to absorb and to exploit, than there was in societies that were more confined, repressive, and exclusive? Is the modern adult capable of managing the residues of infancy without benefit of politicians, bureaucrats, and clergy? These questions require systems theorists to work with social-psychological and psychoanalytic concepts and methods if the field is to move beyond the perennial debates on secularization that rely on Durkheimian and Weberian axioms.

The Dread of Unsatisfied Debt

Let me put forward an "outrageous hypothesis": that postmodern American society is beset by a fear that this country will have to pay the consequences for self-assertion, luxury, and greed. For instance, there may be a widespread, popular, and not wholly unconscious apprehension that one must make sacrifices of the will in order to avert the terrible consequences of triumph and success—a feeling that one may have to pay for one's triumphs, even the imagined ones. That consciousness may be visible in apocalyptic hopes and fears of a final rapture and Armageddon. The same consciousness may take the form of a masochistic social character. Consider Reik's argument:

> There is such a taboo-fear, such a profound unconscious
> dread of a retaliating or revenging power of fate, hidden in
> the masochistic character, similar to the Greeks' fear of
> Hybris . . . Under its pressure the masochist submits . . . to
> all afflictions [in the confidence] that the suffering will bring
> the reward. The anticipation of punishment clears the path
> to the fulfillment of the wishes. (Reik 1957:318–319)

The question is where this sense of dread has gone. As I
have noted, critics, journalists, and the entertainment
industry keep alive at least the rhetoric, and some of the
imagery, of dread; the evangelical wing still proclaims a
day of awesome accounting for the greed and destructiveness in social life and the human heart. *No doubt
these aspects of American society often seem periph-
eral to the decisions of courts and the policy of modern corporations. Nonetheless, these residues and
vestiges of antiquity's sense of dread underlie a masochistic character seeking punishment to atone for destructive motives that are often disguised and yet
occasionally break through to the surface of American
society, especially when greed and destructiveness can
be personified in an external enemy.*
     The optimism of the American nation, its willingness
to believe that it will triumph over all adversities, might
be taken as a sign that Americans as a people are anything but masochistic. However, Reik notes that the masochist is the optimist par excellence. More than anyone
else, the masochist believes that all his or her current
sufferings are nothing, as Paul put it, when compared
with the glory that will be revealed and enjoyed by those
who have endured (see Rom. 8:18). As Reik insists, the
"masochistic character is an unshakable optimist . . .
[and] clings to his hope that the premium for his suffering will come, and he never gives up this hope"
(1957:324). Indeed, the typical American belief, dignified in the so-called civil religion, that Americans will
show other nations the way to truth and virtue (as a

shining light to the nations) is a typically masochist dream of glory. The nation will put others in the shadow by casting its own radiant light. No adversity in the meantime can shake such faith, precisely because its sufferings are the guarantee and sign of eventual victory. So great a triumph over enemies requires corresponding privations along the way as punishments fit for the crime of eventual victory and domination over others. Is the "civil religion" reflected in a national willingness to suffer defeat in Vietnam and incur a crushing national debt? Informed by psychoanalytic concepts, proponents of a "civil religion" hypothesis might look for indicators, at the social-psychological level of observation, in a masochistic social character.

The secularization of modern societies makes it necessary to discern masochistic tendencies that once were more visibly dramatized in religion. Recent studies of Greek antiquity make it obvious that the striving for supremacy, for the conquest of adversity and of adversaries, underlies many a sacrifice, many tragically interrupted and foreshortened lives, and often unspeakable sorrows. In modern societies, however, the dramas of ritual and religious belief in triumph and vindication have been largely muted. Of course, evangelical religion, among others, insists on a day of judgment in which believers' sacrifices will be rewarded and their earthly humiliations reversed. The connection with masochism is apparent in the dream of such vindictive glory and in the use of the term "rapture," which hints at orgiastic rewards to the faithful. Whether the masochistic dream of eventual glory is shifted from this life to posterity, from vindication before an earthly court to the decision of posterity, or even from posterity to a divine tribunal on the last day of judgment, the connection with masochistic fantasies of triumphant retribution is easy to establish (cf. Reik 1957:335–337).

In a secular world, where these grandiose fantasies are

difficult to locate outside what is left of the religious imagination, it may be possible to find traces and signs of social masochism only in the dogged determination and hope against hope of the incurable optimist. If optimism is the American virtue and pessimism the American sin, the underlying masochistic character may still remain, despite secular appearances to the contrary.

The healthy pride of an autonomous individual who gets done what he or she wishes to accomplish is augmented by the pride of the triumphant masochist who succeeds without owing anyone anything. The self-made man or woman without a debt to society, the American ideal, may be a masochist in secular clothing. The workaholic who is modest in success and pays all bills on time fears no reprisals from the less successful or from revenue-seeking institutions like the church and the state. The middle-class masochist thus becomes a secular saint (cf. Reik 1957:390–391).

The masochist, according to Reik (1957:57), engages in acting out his or her fantasies; there is something incurably, essentially theatrical about the masochist. That is why Greek tragedy becomes an elaborate institution in Greek culture; the agonies are protracted, the gods are appeased, and the fates administer their blows of fortune. In the absence of such theater, however, the fantasy goes underground; it becomes a pervasive tendency and affects every aspect of social life without becoming explicit in any theatrical display. This transition from an obvious symptom to a social character typifies the difference between traditional societies, Greek antiquity in particular, and modern societies. In the latter, the elements of fantasy and exhibitionism are still available, but they seem disconnected and are often superficially positive. The nation harbors dreams of enlightening the less fortunate nations of the world by its own victorious and virtuous institutions. Individuals go public with their stories of drug addiction, mental aberration, or operations of one sort or another. There are ample illustrations of masochistic tendencies in American society; what has been lost is the theater that would make them part of an intelligible myth like the "civil religion." The centralizing focus of tragedy and of the liturgy has been replaced by more subtle, chronic, and pervasive tendencies to prolong suffering on the way to the eventual "rapture."

According to my "outrageous hypothesis," these tendencies may create a demand for a day of national suffering followed by national vindication. To live in dread of such a day of judgment may therefore be a pervasive, if not wholly conscious, predisposition in complex societies such as that of the United States. *Secularization deprives sin of its public dramatizations, its articulation in collective myth, without removing the predisposition to guilt and masochism from social character.*

The phenomenon of dread mixes the desire for satisfaction with the fear of a calamity; explosions of anger can be satisfying and frightening, since they may leave nothing and no one standing in their aftermath. No wonder that the apocalypse is both longed for and postponed. For instance, obsessives may long for independence but postpone the day of separation for fear that, in parting, an important part (the "better half") of the self will be left behind and lost forever. There are many reasons why partings are sorrowful as well as sweet, why victories are rewarding and yet full of danger, and why consumption may bring both comfort and danger. The oedipal myth combines elements of victory and tragedy, but so do other myths, for example, the myth of Daedalus and Icarus. It is psychically dangerous to succeed in life where success means taking the place of someone else. Because life is lived at others' expense, the masochist seeks to combine partial satisfaction with partial payment of the debt owed to the living or the dead. There is a certain dread of leaving such a debt unpaid, that the masochist knows too well.

Reik (1957:59–71) argues that the masochist makes these partial payments and enjoys such partial satisfactions in order to ward off dread of a real consummation, of a final victory, and of total satisfaction. The masochist acts in the present "as if" the final satisfaction were being enjoyed in part; that is why there is some pleasure in the anxiety of the masochist. The same way of acting "as if" the future were at hand allows the masochist to ward off and confront the final danger of death and annihilation in small ways, in symbolic gestures, rather than in a final confrontation. Anxiety comes in manageable doses, like pleasure itself. The comparison with religious ritual is explicit and intentional. There is more than an analogy here; I am suggesting that ritual itself is masochistic in the sense that it allows the individual to mix the future with the present in ways that mitigate anxiety and allow small, nonthreatening levels of satisfaction and triumph. The action "as if" the future were at hand means that the triumphs are mock; indeed, the social masochist, freed from the more painful rituals of the clearly neurotic, engages in self-mockery and in mocking various establishments in a provocative, semitheatrical fashion.

5

The Concept of Dread

Dread arises from what Balint (1979) calls the "basic fault." That fault reflects the loss of a world that seemed in infancy to be part of the self: a relationship so basic as to seem an identity rather than a relation. The fault lies deep within, in one's inability to call one's soul one's own. This is also Reik's (1957:76): that even the most masochistic strategies, however self-defeating they may be, are a despairing and distorted struggle of the will to assert itself, to be declared victorious at last, and to be recognized as victor and as something of value by the witnesses to that struggle. The "basic fault" is the inability to feel oneself fully alive, whole, and distinct. That is why the individual seeking to recover himself or herself in analysis needs reassurances of the analyst's immediate, deep, intuitive appreciation and understanding of the individual's feelings beyond—or prior to—the use of words, in the manner of the mutual intermingling of fluids between the fetus and the mother.

The same need to show what is within the self and to have it confirmed by others leads the masochist to act out his or her feelings. In fact, Reik (1957:72ff.) calls this the "demonstrative" aspect of masochism and considers it essential to the concept itself. The desire to "show them" leads to histrionics, to theater and dramatic expressions; it also is tinged with aggressive impulses, as in the conventional expression "I'll show them." This dream of glory, to show them (up), underlies the masochist's fantasies of victory and retribution and permeates the national dreams of entire peoples for a millennial or apocalyptic triumph. The fault thus being demonstrated is an original one: universal, profound, and recurrent. What varies is the social form it takes: the masochism of the individual, the self-destructive and aggressive demonstrations of religious communities like Jonestown, the ethnic demonstrations of the Palestinian intifadah that lead to further humiliation and suffering for the powerless, or the more dreadful holocaust of an entire people sure of their ultimate vindication.

Perennial, Chronic Dread

Not all dread, of course, is so intense. Rank (1950) argues that there is an underlying, chronic, and universal dread in the human condition regardless of whether one lives in a primitive or a complex, a traditional or a modern, society. In an attempt to ward off the fear of death, one limits one's consumption, avoids risks, and lives, therefore, a relatively constricted existence. Such an approach reminds one of the child who avoids stepping on cracks to avoid breaking his or her mother's back. On the other hand, the constricted life that results is one of missed opportunities; the individual also experiences the dread of having failed to keep an important appointment with life, as it were. In the interplay between these two forms of anxiety, one over death and one over life, there is room for the development of culture, whether that be the culture of the Greek tragedy, the conflict between charismatic leaders and officials, or the constant comment of journalists and preachers in modern societies. *My first proposition, then, is that there is a perennial, chronic, low-intensity dread of that results from the interaction between life-anxiety and death-anxiety.* The proposition can be specified for particular societies, so that in antiquity one might examine the major rites and dramas, whereas in modern societies one might examine, for instance, public rhetoric, the popular wisdom literature, and secular entertainment.

Dread is least intense when individuals seek to avoid death by limiting their experience and enjoyment of life. At its most intense, one can see precisely this bargain with death: a magical effort to ward off death by depriving oneself of movement, exposure, satisfaction, and mastery. In their review of forty-two cases at the Menninger Clinic over the last thirty years, Wallerstein and his associates (1986:122ff.) found eighteen with anxieties that "had crystallized into clear phobic attitudes and/or symptoms." One of them, for instance, had learned of her father's heart attack on a sunny day and had developed a fear of bright days, as if by avoiding the sunlight she could ward off the threat of death to her father (and no doubt also to herself). She went on to constrict her life in other ways, from overeating to avoiding small enclosures, like elevators. The constrictions multiplied as she shut herself off from life in order to avoid confronting her more fundamental fear. On the other hand, some patients seemed to be quite free of the constrictions imposed by civilization on the expression of anger and hatred. They freely savaged and bludgeoned their rivals, had tantrums, drove dangerously, or incapacitated themselves with their own rage, as in the case of a woman whose outbursts were marked by fear of being killed by her husband or of her own suicide. One, "the Economist," constantly fearful of being assaulted, always carried a pistol and a club in his car in order to be properly vigilant against attack" (Wallerstein 1986:125). Some lived in fear of life in order to avoid death; others lived in fear of death in order to avoid owning and controlling their most aggressive impulses, drives that otherwise could give them extraordinary vital energy. These are the compromises that cause symptoms; they are also the compromises that create culture. Indeed, culture allows individuals to live with a good conscience within the compromises valued by their societies.

That is also Rank's (1971) point about sacrifices of the will. These sacrifices allow the individual to live within the terms offered by a society, terms that promise the soul a measure of immortality in return for a constricted life. That life is to be lived, however, entirely within whatever boundaries the society requires for its citizens. Those who live life outside the bounds of civility, the aggressive types just mentioned, have the makings of Genghis Khans or desperadoes. Only in relatively rare cases do they transform their notoriety into something enshrined in cultural memory. Their victories in life deprive them of their place at the center of a society's values. Desperadoes are seldom buried at Westminster Abbey, although the people who admired and loved them may go on pilgrimage to their shrines in the countryside. It is the choice between "doing it my way" and Graceland, on the one hand, and, on the other, burial at Arlington Cemetery or one's name carved on the black rock of the Vietnam War Memorial.

In societies that act out these dilemmas in ritual and on stage, there is no doubt about the compromise that the society prefers. The triumph of good over evil, of life over death, of the soul of the ancestors over the will of the recalcitrant individual—all these are achieved at a certain cost or sacrifice after a long and determined struggle by the heroes and protagonists. In a society such as the United States, however, there is no central stage that offers a place to dramatize these dilemmas, no single myth that defines the hero and calls for sacrifice.

Of course, the courts and the mass media try to transform the events of everyday life into the semblance, if not the very stuff, of ritual and drama. In New York City Bernhard Goetz, like the Economist in the example just given, lived in fear and walked about armed and ready for struggle. His story resonated with thousands of citi-

zens who, similarly ready to act out their aggressive impulses, saw in him their hero or their fate. Conversely,
like the phobic patients who lived in darkness and constricted their lives in various ways, Tawana Brawley's
self-immolation and reclusive life resonated with every
fearful person who, if not actually phobic, understood
the effort to ward off the threat of attack and of death by
a constriction of life. In the press and on the television
news, these events and actors became protagonists in the
universal dilemmas pitting life against death.

I am suggesting that at the basis of ordinary, everyday
social life is what Wallerstein (1986:287) calls a transference "jam" or even a transference "neurosis." Feelings that come from an early moment in the person's life
are "transferred" to the present. In analysis, the analyst
is the recipient of these feelings; in the larger society,
however, there is literally no limit to the objects that
can be the recipients of transference. Patients willingly
constrict their lives by transferring certain childhood
feelings to their analysts. They avoid confronting their
own mortality. They imagine themselves to be in the
presence of a responsive and nurturing mother at the
cost, however, of failing to discover their own sources of
nourishment. They feel themselves indebted for their
very lives to their analysts, at the cost of becoming more
creative themselves. All these costs occur within the
limitations of the analytic discipline and routine.

Some patients, as Wallerstein frequently notes, fail to
leave this transference situation. Many of them also lead
highly constricted lives in the everyday world—in their
homes, at work, and even in their leisure activities. Indeed, some of the patients who failed to abandon their
transference neurosis or "jam" were reported years later
to be living out the same routines as when they entered
analysis: visiting parents, working too hard on the job,
waiting patiently for spouses, and so on. The dread of a
full life and of death itself causes these expatients to stay

within well-worn social tracks, in which they are rewarded for their work and devotion; despite these rewards, the sense of owing the self or someone else an
unpaid debt remains. Shortchanged by life and by psychoanalysis, they fail to realize that they have shortchanged themselves. My first proposition therefore
suggests that such compromises are attempts to ward off
an existential dread that is far more widespread than
these examples from the clinic might suggest.

Other sources of dread lie in grandiose (and infantile)
notions of one's importance. Grandiosity among adults
wears many faces, and that is why it is so difficult to identify. Some faces represent ideals: idealistic pictures of
one's community, one's friends and family, one's position
in society, or one's nation itself. It is one's own self-love
and demand for credit, however, that underlies such ide-
alism. When one's ideals are betrayed, therefore, one becomes hungry for recognition and exceedingly suspicious
of the greed of those who have failed one.

Other grandiose faces wear the mask of life, so to
speak, to conceal the fact of one's own inevitable death.
These are faces of people with whom one identifies. In
identifying with them one seems to guarantee not just
one's own importance but life itself (just as the infant
anchors its soul in the face of the parent). When the
mask fails, so to speak, one sees the face from which one
is hiding, one's mortal self. One then receives another
wound to one's imaginary and grandiose side.

Finally, grandiosity may come back to haunt in other
ways. If one has been unconsciously devouring those
whom one desires (or desires to eliminate), one may
well feel anxious about the thoughts that these others
may have of one; one becomes unduly beholden to the
expectations and judgments of others in the community.
One imagines these others to have a consuming interest
in oneself, and one may feel unduly obligated to account
for oneself to the community. These grandiose images

may inspire or intimidate, frighten or embolden, in one's own imaginary social world if they develop into a "phantasy social system" (Bion 1957).

Dread of Increasing Intensity

A chronic level of low-intensity dread may therefore underlie modern societies, where sin, being secularized, is relatively free-floating. Under certain conditions, however, dread can focus on the community or society itself. An axiom of Durkheimian sociology, for instance, is that societies produce ideal representations of themselves that inspire a certain awe; sociologists in the Weberian tradition, however, are more likely to regard these images or representations as ersatz, a halo that gives modern political institutions or the nation a glory fabricated from romantic attachments to previous forms of social life like the community or the clan. (The differences between these two viewpoints cannot be resolved empirically, that is, by studying the conditions conducive to idealizing the larger society. This is because Weber and Durkheim differed on what they took to be real about social life: the individual as bedrock or society itself as ontologically prior to the individual). Nonetheless, in the difference between these two views, there is room for a question about the degree to which individuals in a particular society idealize that society or remain indifferent or even suspicious of it. That question is one that can be answered by observation. I would suggest that, as *a second proposition, dread increases in intensity when the individual withdraws his or her emotional investment from that society.* The proposition clearly runs counter to Durkheim's insistence that individuals live in awe of societies that represent their ideals; I have derived this proposition from Freud's notion of "dread of the community," to which I now turn.

What Freud means by "dread of the community" in-

cludes guilt: one's feeling that one has failed to live up
to an ideal self. That ideal may be a social one, and its
loss is painful, to say the least. Because that ideal was
based on self-love, individuals lick the wounds to their
collective self-esteem and revert to more private, self-
oriented forms of love. This withdrawal of affection from
the community leads to dread, however, that others will
administer suitable punishment to the individual. The
most fitting punishment for the crime of withdrawing
love from the family, community, or nation would be for
the community to withdraw its love from the individual.
This correspondence of crime and punishment follows
Freud's notion of the *lex talionis,* the eye-for-an-eye mentality that makes each psychological self-punishment fit
the psychic crime. Here is the way Freud put it: "Originally this was . . . the dread of losing their [the parents']
love; later the parents are replaced by an indefinite number of fellow-men. This helps us understand why it is that
paranoia is frequently caused by a wounding of the ego"
(1975:59).

Dread of the community, then, is partly anxiety that
the community, like the vengeful parent, will punish
the child for living at the expense of the world on which
the child depends for sustenance and life itself.

Licking that wound takes away some of the pain. Such
lavish and loving attention to the self's imaginary
wounds also takes away an individual's affection from
the world. It is really this withdrawal of interest and
affection that produces what Freud calls "dread of the
community." The later, "wounded" form of narcissistic
love comes with guilt, since "it has doubtless come into
being at the expense of the object-libido" (Freud
1975:32).

In secular societies a somewhat more diffuse dread of
the community, a pervasive sense of guilt, comes from
the individual's withdrawal of emotional investment in
the community. Wounds to the individual's self-esteem

come when an overestimated community (family or nation) loses its imagined value. Individuals then become preoccupied with assuaging their losses of self-esteem and with making themselves feel better. Unfortunately, this lavish expenditure of affection on the self costs the community its share of the individual's self-love, and in the economy of the unconscious, someone must pay for withdrawing these deposits of affection—the one who makes the withdrawal. Hence the individual's dread of the community is the result of expecting punishment for the individual's own, prior rejection of, and withdrawal from, the community itself.

When affection is withdrawn, Freud tells us, sadness rather than protest is often the result—that is, the sin of melancholy.

> The occasions giving rise to melancholia for the most part extend beyond the clear case of a loss by death, and include all those situations of being wounded, hurt, neglected, out of favour, or disappointed, which can import opposite feelings of love and hate into a relationship or reinforce an already existing ambivalence. (1975:161)

Freud (1975:160) also points out that even when some love is withdrawn from an object, the object (person, community, ideal) may be taken into the self in some way. The vicious circle thus begins with the individual's feeling of "being wounded, hurt, neglected, out of favour, or disappointed," to reiterate Freud's list of insults to the person's self-importance. In the next stage the individual withdraws some of the affection for the self that had been invested in a part of the world, only to feel guilty for making that withdrawal. One begins to dread punishment for having withdrawn the initial deposit of affection. Now, the circle can go beyond a vague uneasiness about the community; the individual, imagining that the community feels jilted and punitive, may feel disapproving toward the community that is still part of the self. Such disapproval of the internal community leads to self-recrimination and possibly even to depression or to paranoia, when the individual feels apprehensive that the community, still "swallowed," may become a source of persecution. Not everything one swallows, in the sense of psychological consumption, is digestible or benign. Once one feels persecuted by internal sources of recrimination, there may well be a temptation to disown those parts of the self that are sensed to be the source of one's chronic indigestion, so to speak.

Psychiatrists who work in the tradition of Melanie Klein have much to say about the interplay between projected and introjected parts of the self, an interaction that may lead some to depression and others to more paranoid fears and schizoid techniques of ridding the self of internal torment. Dread, as a secularized sense of sin, can focus outward on the community or inward on the self. Focused outward, dread senses strange or possibly dangerous places in the community and fears retaliation or rejection from parts of the community; focused inward, dread becomes sadness over the loss of a world of some integrity and beauty.

Freud also makes it very clear that mourning and melancholy have much in common, and also that they differ from each other at one important point. Those who mourn are quite conscious of what they have lost, whether that is a person or some ideal that stood originally for a person, the fatherland, or the alma mater (Freud 1975:155). True melancholy shifts the focus of reproach onto the self, whereas "the fall in self-esteem is absent in grief" (Freud 1975:153). Dread thus becomes abhorrence of an evil within: an unpaid debt to some aspect of the self.

That is why Melanie Klein thought that "taking in and expelling" may be "at the bottom of all our complicated dealings with one another" (Klein, quoted in Jaques

1957:481). The sense of an unpaid debt comes from "investing" and "depositing" the self in others and from the consuming passions that tie people both to one another and to specific places. The debt is most serious when there is a nearly organic connection between people or between people and institutions. When that connection remains largely unconscious, however, it can cause considerable anxiety.

Psychological debt is therefore a two-way street. To consume is to destroy the other; to invest the self in someone else is to be consumed, absorbed by them. We speak of being attached to or absorbed by another person or a place; we have absorbing interests, in which it is we who are taken in and ingested by a novel or play. The technical terms of projection and introjection serve nicely to distinguish who is consuming or being consumed.

If Klein is right, these projections have been going on since childhood, when the child attributes his or her greedy and loving impulses to a mother who can then be reabsorbed (introjected) into the child, the "good" along with the "bad": "Identification by projection implies a combination of splitting off parts of the self and projecting them onto (or rather into) another person" (1957a: 311–312). What is projected may be the nourished or the empty parts of the self, the strong aspects of the self or the weak, the full or the depleted. The mother, thus imagined as more or less devoured, either in bits or nourishing and complete, is then taken back into the infant's self. The resulting internal experience of the child can therefore be full of contradictions: wholeness and being-in-pieces, fullness and emptiness, abundance and scarcity. In fact, what the infant has done in imagination may seem uniquely realistic, as if the child actually has consumed, wasted, or otherwise devoured the mother. The resulting emotions are disturbing, as Klein notes: "This entails sorrow and guilt

about the harm done [in omnipotent fantasies] to an object which is now felt to be both loved and hated; these
anxieties and the defenses against them represent the
depressive positions" (1957a:312). All this imaginary
taking in and putting out of the other is really just a
putting out and taking in of parts of the self that one
attributes or lends to others. It can seem to the unconscious, where the individual's powers no longer feel
imaginary but real and omnipotent, as though one were
largely responsible for the fate of others. Such a sense of
responsibility can be experienced as a terrible debt that
can only be paid at great cost to the self, if it can be paid
at all.

As Klein's observations suggest, dread is intensified
when there is a certain confusion of boundaries between
the self and the world around. There is no such confusion in the relatively lower degrees of intensity of dread
that I have already discussed; the self is aware of existential dilemmas in a world that is quite distinct from the
person concerned. The world is full of irreconcilable
choices and incommensurate alternatives between living
and dying. The second proposition thus concerned an
intensity of dread that assumes the development of a self
separate enough from the world to make emotional investments in it and to withdraw them. The relation is
narcissistic, since the social world is still a reflection
of—or on—the self, a narcissism that some writers
would call secondary.

Dread of Being

Primary narcissism is what concerns me now, as I suggest *a third proposition: When the ego is relatively
undifferentiated from the social world, the self will experience a dread of its own being, an original sin.*
Under certain social conditions, the self is necessarily
confused with its social environment, not only in in-

fancy but also in entire societies that enforce through ritual and myth the most profound and complex intermingling of the self with others. Under these conditions, individuals will become convinced that they are tainted with some basic or fatal flaw. The flaw may be called an original sin, or it may be attributed to the internal presence of impure and hateful spirits of which the self would like to be rid once and for all. In the records of modern psychiatry, the flaw may be simply acknowledged by a patient as just that: nothing mythic, but simply a fault, like the San Andreas, that runs through and cuts across the self at its deepest level. Myth makes the basic fault inevitable and universal. Modern psychiatry treats it as an aspect of personal development and history.

Although I have been speaking of the maternal space in quite literal terms, that is, in terms of the womb, the infant experiences a much wider range or people and circumstances as the maternal space. All those caring for the infant constitute the space that the child used to encounter when in the womb. If those people are abrupt or uncaring, unpredictable or suffocating, in their care, the infant knows only that he or she does not fit in. It is the feeling of fitting in that makes the child's experience of care after birth seem, as it were, *fitting*. There are many reasons why the child may not fit in, over and above the failings of the parents and other caregivers; that is not my point here. There is, for a wide variety of reasons, when care is deficient, what Balint calls

> a lack of "fit" between the child and *the people* who represent his [*sic*] environment. . . . It is definitely a two-person relationship in which, however, only one person matters; his wishes and needs are the only ones that count and must be attended to; the other partner, though felt to be immensely powerful, matters only insofar as he is willing to gratify his first partner's needs and desires or decides to frustrate them. (Balint 1979:22–23)

In this primary relationship, any disruption is experienced as a fundamental flaw in the self, since the self expands to fit the "maternal space" provided by the infant's earliest social world. As Balint (1979) reminds us, that sense of a "basic fault" may permeate all aspects of the child's later life and run through every stage of later development. There it will be experienced as a variety of failings, an inability to fit in, a sense of being fundamentally deficient and incomplete; a patient, for instance, "feels that there is a fault within him, a fault that must be put right. . . . Second, there is a feeling that the cause of this fault is that someone has either failed the patient or defaulted on him" (Balint 1979:21).

Note how primitive this sense of indebtedness really is. It is a sense that the patient owes—and is owed— something beyond ordinary reckoning; someone has defaulted on the patient, and the patient also is faulty. The debt is primitive because the distinction between the self and the world is blurred; it is not clear who has defaulted on whom. It is a primitive debt because the sense of "someone" and "something" being owed underlies so much of later life, of mental conflicts, and of physical ills. Mythologized, the fault becomes a dreaded fate or an original sin that requires lifelong payment on an unspeakable debt. Without the trappings of myth, the object of dread remains diffuse, and the terms of payment are never settled.

There are two aspects of this basic fault. One has to do with a flawed relation to others in the world. Those who seem most desirable and important always seem just beyond reach, in a class by themselves—objects to be adored rather than enjoyed or mastered. There is a danger, as Balint (1979) repeatedly observes, that the analyst will become such an object; the patient will always feel that there is a gulf fixed between him or her and the analyst that cannot be crossed. The religious sense of devotion perpetuates such a feeling. Devotion, like the patient's admiration for the analyst, can lead the devotee to feel permanently outclassed, wholly unworthy to be in the company of the god in question. All one can do, therefore, is to sacrifice with feelings of pleasure and remorse—with satisfaction that one's gift is being received, yet with dissatisfaction with a gift that can only be second best.

The best, by definition, is outside oneself in the god who is willing to be considered omniscient and omnipotent. Devotion, like addiction, therefore has pleasant but temporary side effects and long-term, disabling consequences. In the end, one knows for certain that one cannot span the distance separating heaven from earth. Complex societies multiply the objects of admiration and the avenues for devotion; pilgrimage can focus on occupational or political goals; it may become entirely an individual pursuit of private goals. The coach of Notre Dame's football team claims to have reached 85 of 107 of his personal objects of devotion. His goals, besides being Notre Dame's coach, include owning a 1949 Chevrolet (he does) and going for a cruise on a submarine (a goal not yet achieved) (*Wall Street Journal,* Dec. 27, 1988:1).

There is another aspect of this basic flaw, one even more painful than the first. Balint speaks of a state of "regret" or of "mourning"; it is about the unalterable fact of a defect or a fault in oneself that, in fact, has cast its shadow over one's whole life, and the unfortunate effects of which can never fully "be made good" (1979:183). The regret stems from the very fact of a deficiency in one's self, the "basic fault" of which Balint speaks. The fault lies not only in one's distance from a person like one's mother, who was life itself to one during infancy. The fault lies in a space that one never could fill: the maternal space that remains perpetually empty and unfulfilled. The space may be a place of importance in the lives of others; it may be a potential that remains unfulfilled or an opportunity not taken. There are words not spoken, an emptiness created by the loss of words or by the sheer inadequacy of language.

If the first aspect of this basic fault is an "unbridgeable gulf," the second is therefore an emptiness unfilled by one's own self. That is why Balint, in the passage just quoted, speaks of fault or a defect that can never be made good. A complex society provides a multiplicity of spaces that one can fill and so makes use of the desire to fill such an empty place and cure one's fault, but these spaces can be filled by anyone who qualifies. Sole and permanent occupancy is denied everyone. The fault is never wholly cured, and dread of losing one's space becomes endemic, chronic, and part of a common fate that remains a matter of fact rather than mythic.

In a society premised and organized on religious terms, the desire for such unconditional and endless love can be focused on the Deity. In Christian terms, such a deity's love is just that: eternal, without condition. It is the cure for sin, because it comes with an empathy and understanding for protracted, seemingly hopeless personal suffering. As such it perpetuates the type of unresolvable "transference neurosis" that Wallerstein (1986:302ff.) found in several patients, dubbed "hysterical" for clinical reasons. Each of these found their analyses partially successful precisely because they seemed to promise this primordial satisfaction: the "harmonious mix" that many of Balint's more intractable patients unconsciously desired, as though the relationship with the analyst could provide the firm but flexible support and nurturance of the womb or—later—the breast. The same analyses eventually failed, although they at first appeared to succeed. The analysts found themselves unable to work through with the patient the underlying desire for endless, limitless love.

Balint therefore argues that the technique of analysis, heavily dependent on interpretive language, is most effective in dealing with oedipal rather than pre-oedipal and preverbal strains of the patient's experience. Indeed, Wallerstein (1986:320) finds in one case a similar preference on the part of the analyst for focusing on oedipal strivings; it left the patient's deeper yearnings for a relationship with her mother relatively unexamined. There was mourning in such cases for the terminated analysis, but such mourning was far less helpful than mourning for the unrealistic possibility of heaven on earth, that is, for the "harmonious mix" that Balint describes. Without such mourning, patients are left with a sense of having a basic fault. For instance, one patient with an incomplete analysis at the Menninger Foundation went through the rest of her life feeling hopelessly flawed: "indecisively spinning her wheels in what often seemed like a bleak and effortful life struggle" (Wallerstein 1968:318–319). There is here a tragic and chronic, low-level rather than intense sense of an unfulfilled promise—a debt to the self that can never be paid in full.

Thus several forms of dread may cluster in the masochistic character, as Reik describes it. Certainly there are narcissistic underpinnings; the masochist feels "he has paid by his suffering for his spiritual sins and thus has been entitled to a delayed premium" (Reik 1957:334). This is the secondary narcissism of imaginary entitlements, but it is based on an earlier, primary form of narcissism that demands the fulfillment of one's wishes: the primitive will of the infant that later becomes the determined character of the masochist. There is also a trace of the obsessive neurosis in masochism; both the obsessive and the masochist envisage some dire calamity in the future. While the masochist may be taking active steps to pay for the damages inflicted unconsciously on others, the obsessive may be equally apprehensive but perhaps more passive in warding off disaster. In both there is an atrophy of the will, as the individual's energies are spent in ways that perpetuate frustration and delay satisfaction. In societies that demand long delays in satisfaction in return for opportunities for self-advancement, an obsessive-masochist character, full of determination and with a high sense of responsibility, may become widespread without the stimulus of ritual and the moral guidance of a priesthood that wants the laity to be like priests.

The traces of an even earlier stage of development are apparent in the masochistic character. This is the time when the infant could not distinguish between the self and others; the person punished is merged in the infant's mind with the self doing the punishing. It is as if in the dream of annihilating the frustrating parent or hated rival the dreaming child could not distinguish between himself or herself and the figures in the dream. That indeed is the way with dreams, and it is part and parcel of the earliest, infantile imagination. Finally, the guilt of the masochist may stem from the feeling that one's existence is flawed because it is insufficiently separated from other selves that are both feared and loved, desired and hated. Even in the masochistic character that works hard, uses credit reasonably, pays bills on time, and seeks insurance against calamities, there may well be profound, quasi-neurotic forms of dread. The more "normal" such a character becomes, the less will such a psychological predisposition to social obligation require the supports of myth and ritual.

When one invests the "good" or "bad" parts of the self in leaders, a place, or an institution, the parts of the self that are felt to be good are often split from the parts of the self that are felt to be bad. Both are projected (i.e., invested or deposited) into quite different institutions or places in different friends or leaders. When the process goes far enough, individuals can no longer recognize or retrieve what they have invested in others. The self, to that extent, has already been lost; the individual has already suffered a genuine loss of self. Conscious efforts can then be spent to recover a self that is estranged by having become unconscious, dissociated (the good from the bad), and projected outward. The attempt to recover these lost parts of the self can lead the individual to internalize what was projected: to confuse the self with its own shadow. That is why Jaques finds that social institutions, as repositories of the self, become "internal defences against anxiety, and guilt" (1957:481). As defenses they become substitutes for the true self, which is lost in its many disguises and projections.

Splitting, whether projecting or dividing up the self, therefore involves a very real loss of the self. Klein (1957a:337) discusses a literary character who has a strong "feeling of guilt about having neglected and deserted a precious component of the personality." He or she has "the urge to regain his [*sic*] former self" and the "longing to be himself [*sic*] again" (Klein 1957a:337). Klein singles out this character, whose story reads like a series of projections and introjections; the character in question is repeatedly investing herself in others, absorbing others into herself, and feels constantly troubled by these other presences in her life. She is also troubled by the inevitable partings and is concerned about the fate of her former identifications. It becomes clear that the person who has been abandoned is the character herself, that is, her true self.

To lose the capacity to act on one's own behalf is a frightening thing. Some fear paralysis and imprisonment; others fear the inability to find the right words, to reach a destination, or to find and save someone they love. This nightmare has many forms, but the underlying dread is the same: a pervasive and relentless fear of losing one's innermost self, one's will or soul. It is a fear that always comes true for everyone in death itself; in death one does indeed lose one's will, one's very self. It is understandable that so many kinds of religious beliefs and practices seek to guarantee the survival or rebirth of the soul. It is also not surprising that individuals who feel depressed experience emptiness and a loss of will-power. No wonder they fear that their reserves of time, energy, and other resources are running low.

Dread of losing one's soul is like the "sting of death"; sin is thus a reminder of what is to come and a foretaste of the eventual loss of one's very self. Indeed, the borderline between life and death seems somewhat tenuous for an individual who is experiencing a partial paralysis of will; as Rank points out concerning Hamlet, to possess one's own soul requires that one be able to act decisively on one's own behalf, even in the face of death, rather than to debate the relative merits of life and death. Rank argues that Hamlet "was finally able to achieve blood vengeance because he could then act in self-defense and on his own will, instead of in obedience to his father. This developmental step resolves the whole problem of will and fate, and of procreation and individualization" (1950:66).

To take decisive action, to recover one's own soul from a state of paralysis, it is psychologically necessary (Rank argues) to incur an unavoidable, even incurable guilt. That is why so many heroes die in their search for immortality. The enemy is always the same, that is, the knowledge of one's own eventual death. Rank argues that in slaying Abel, Cain was killing the knowledge of his own mortality. Abel represented the old immortal soul, while "Cain represented the first man born of woman to lose the spiritual immortality which Abel embodied" (Rank 1950:156). That is why Abel had to die; he was the offensive reminder of what Cain had lost (immortality) and of what he must face, that is, that his own life is purchased at the price of death. To be able to act decisively, then, and to exact the payment oneself are necessary if one is to recover one's will and restore one's own soul, but the price is a guilt that cannot be assuaged.

There are a large number of gods that humankind has created to guarantee the immortality of the soul. According to Rank, each demands a sacrifice of the will that gave birth to the god in question. In other words, every Cain seeks to create an Abel, but Abel reminds Cain of the immortality that Cain has thus surrendered to his image: the first deified figment of his imagination. Rank indeed has quite a list of such "gods" or cultural fictions. There are gods who are bad because they personify human destructive impulses, and good gods who protect humans from bad ones. There are gods of the unabashed will, like father-gods who personify one's desire to be the source of one's own life, but these father-gods in turn demand sacrifices. Therefore one creates mother-gods who personify divine love to protect one from the father, but mother-gods create their own demands for obedience and self-surrender. One therefore returns to the original imaginary self with divine claims to immortality and power. Self-deification emerges only in the final stages of the creative imagination or in cultural history; it was present, however, at human origins and appears at various times and places in the development of the individual (Rank 1936). Individualism is not a modern disease, despite the usual diatribe of conservative sociology. What is new is that individual self-deification no longer is defined entirely by religious myth or requires the services of the clergy to be part of *la vie serieuse.*

The point is that an individual will sacrifice his or her own sense of willpower to avoid the dread of having an impossible debt to pay. Such a debt reflects the incurable guilt that comes from isolating or withdrawing the self from the social pressures that burden one's fellow citizens. That isolation, however, can be creative rather than pathological (cf. Rank 1936:81). This fourth, most intense form of dread is the experience of survivors who have escaped the burdens and penalties that others have suffered. For instance, others may have died while one still lives and moves freely, or others may have sacrificed to the gods of normalcy while one has enjoyed comparative freedom, and even the illicit pleasures of taking revenge. This form of dread may result in a feeling of obligation, a feeling that one owes someone or something a debt that can never be paid, because one has not sacrificed those desires and surrendered that will to some external sources of judgment in the courts or the community. Perhaps one has missed the opportunity to save others, that is, failed to act when one could have, in order either to satisfy some moral standard or to save oneself from condemnation. The opportunities that one has missed and the pain one has failed to avert, when one might otherwise have acted effectively, are the stuff around which obsessions grow. One reminisces about love lost or injuries and death that one has failed to prevent; one is haunted by the words one has failed to speak. The combination of such losses and responsibilities underlies this sense of guilt, which is perhaps the most visible aspect or level of dread.

Dread When Ritual Fails

In many respects the experience of survivors of disasters will be the same whether the disaster occurred in the first or the twentieth century. There is an aspect of grief that is perennial, although the forms of mourning may radically differ from one society to another. That is precisely the point of my next suggestion. *As a fourth proposition, I would suggest that dread will be most pervasive and identifiable among those whose rituals fail to express and resolve a sense of guilt at being released from the burdens that afflict others, especially death.*

What about the experiences of individuals in modern societies? Are we any less tormented than those who still rake through the remains to see what signs there may be of life among the dead? Is our search of the underworld less filled with agony than the search of those in antiquity, who literally trembled and shook as they entered into their mysteries? These are difficult questions, since we have no direct access to the experience of those who actually participated in ancient rites; there is some reason to believe that they took part in them with little conviction or understanding, although some no doubt did experience both agony and exhilaration, joy and sorrow. The same range of experience can be found in Danforth's (1982) photographs of women opening the graves of the dead after five years to exhume the remains: curiosity, distraction, practical interest, eager anticipation, awful sorrow. By comparison, American funeral rites are quick, final, pedestrian; there is no exhumation, no final collection of the remains, no collective ossuary.

There is no end of the studies that remind us that death in the modern West is only a shadow of its former self. The mystery has disappeared along with the collective drama. It is a private thing, except when someone's death rocks the public: Kennedy shot, *Challenger* destroyed, King murdered. Even then, the exhumations occur immediately, the investigations are public, the media spell out the findings day after day. There are no remains left in the underworld of the public consciousness.

That is the point; the routine and the rational now appear to control the guilt that once received more dramatic expression in traditional societies. The desire to recover and restore the dead and the fear of their return have found literally dozens of separate channels. How many thousands of mystery stories are read annually in the United States by how many thousands of people? How many mysteries are watched on the screen or bought on videotape? Simply asking the question is a way of suggesting that the mysteries of antiquity have become the merchandise of popular culture.

It is no accident, therefore, that a revival of interest in original sin accompanied the period of violence in the West from the beginning of the World War I to the disenchantment with Stalin in 1956. Binion attributes the "comeback of original sin . . . to 1956 together with a resurgence of the death-row image of human existence" to the "massive, protracted orgy of brutality and carnage" that included revolution, war, and gulags and death camps and culminated in the slaughter of citizens in Nagasaki and Hiroshima (1986:87). In the literary and theatrical treatment of original sin, however, the doctrinal connection between sin and death was broken. Individuals were mystified by the sentence of death: some unable to find guilt in their hearts, others only too glad to find sin in order to give their death sentence meaning. The connection between action and fate was broken, Binion argues, and the residues of the Christian myth were unable to sustain a sense that this twentieth-century fatality was deserved. For Kafka, who began the writing of *The Trial* immediately after the Austro-Hungarian invasion of Serbia and Russia's mobilization in July 1914, that disaster was as unwarranted as his early expulsion from home by his father. Whatever residues of original sin can be found in *The Trial* are due to a secularized Christian consciousness that still hopes to find some connection between individual guilt and the universal death sentence. If Binion (1986) is right, that is a forlorn hope in a post-Christian world.

Nonetheless, planners and intellectuals continue to try to prevent disasters in the future and to give old ones new meaning. The order of the West depends on rational inquiries into cell life or social history, into disasters and accidents, into the fate of survivors and the sacrifices of those who have no memorial. Higher culture mounts a continuous inquest or inquisition into the causes of life and death, into the fate of anonymous individuals as well as of entire populations. The exhumations continue in the most orderly fashion. They are conducted by specialists in a wide range of fields. The results of the investigations as well as their methods are widely publicized and publicly scrutinized. Modern culture, whether it is popular, specialized, or esoteric, is a vast, careful, routine, and complex expression of the desires that once went into the polishing of gravestones, the exhumation of the dead, the crafting of rites, and the ecstasies of one mystery cult or another.

It is one thing for a society to utilize the guilt that once was directed in ritual toward the dead and the departed; it is quite another to satisfy the longing of the living for the dead. Sublimation of desire only works for a time. That is no doubt why many read mysteries in a modern society that provides so many rational and public channels for inquest and inquiry. Almost thirty years later books are still being written about Kennedy's assassination and about the killing of three civil rights workers in Mississippi. The Warren Commission did not satisfy the public desire for an autopsy with divination; neither did the courts and the press satisfy the public need to take part in the exhumation of the remains of the young men buried beneath that makeshift dam in rural Mississippi. Even so, all these inquiries reduce protest to entertainment. Box office receipts and publishers' earnings in the market for public exhumations continue to go up. The case, whether it is the case of Karen Silkwood or of the Nazi holocaust, is never fully closed. Modern societies thus make use of the dread of guilt and renew each generation's encounters with the past. In doing so, however, they will never satisfy the demand for the truth of the matter—for a resolution of the problem of guilt.

The reason for my "outrageous hypothesis" may now be somewhat clearer. The capacity of modern societies to relieve the dread of guilt is weaker than their ability to make use of such dread for social purposes. We seem to have lost the means to exhume the remains of the departed once and for all. To put the bones in the collective ossuary is to put them away; villages in rural Greece still know how to complete the process of burial. It takes five years, but when it is done, there is no devotion left untapped. No agony remains untold. In modern societies, it would seem, there is no end to the unearthing of the remains of old tragedies. There seems no way to fully tell the tale of past agony; the case is never fully closed. The dread that Melanie Klein has documented concerning persecution by the absent or the departed on their return was relieved by traditional rites. The same dread is now chronic, sublimated into high or mediocre culture but never cured either by eternal love or by the simple truth.

The funeral laments that Danforth (1982) has described in such telling detail are often used at other times of departure in rural Greece. When brides leave their parents' home, they still sing a lament, with few changes in words, to suit the occasion of this new departure. They are not coming back. Their journey takes them into a world from which there is no return, a world of *xenitia,* of foreignness, where they will live and die among strangers. It is like a death, and the laments make the resemblance poignant and clear. I am arguing that the loss of ritualized enactments makes the same transition from one stage in life to the next far more ambiguous, lengthier, and problematic in modern societies, where foreignness has become a way of life.

The constant demand for an exhumation of the past

reflects the inability of a society to enact in ritual the words of a final departure. The Warren Commission adjourns, but the case is not closed. Juries act, but the process of disclosing and reliving the circumstances of a crime is not finished once and for all. The past returns to haunt the present, especially in societies that have changed departure from an event into a process. Devotion to the departed is not exhausted or consumed in any final rite of exhumation. The bones of the past are thus never fully laid to rest.

Sin has become secularized into a form of fear that I would prefer to call dread. It is fear that something terrible will happen. Perhaps one's health or possessions will be taken away; one might even lose one's very life. The term "dread" adds to fear the element of obligation or indebtedness. It is as if the group were saying that the worst will not happen if only the group goes through certain symbolic acts. For instance, if one offers a gift to the gods, whatever one has left will not be taken away—hence the origin of tithing (Burkert 1979:53). The obligation to the gods, once settled symbolically, allows one to enjoy the remaining fruits of one's labors. Dread is thus a reaction to the threat of greed. Either other people will be greedy and seek to take away one's possessions, or else one's own greed will pose a threat to social order. Greed in either case requires a symbolic gesture of renunciation to demonstrate that one is not going to live at others' expense. This gesture is obligatory and pays an implied debt to greed: a sacrifice to demonstrate that greed either has been satisfied or will not destroy one's relationships and the community itself.

There are other kinds of fear alleviated with other kinds of payment. Burkert (1979:50) argues that the experience of fear is fundamental to religious observances in a wide range of cultures. It is fear, however, transformed into something less overwhelming. Instead of becoming paralyzed by a fear of animals or other predators, of sickness, of enemies, and of death, humans have found ways of experiencing and relieving fear in stereotyped symbolic gestures: ritual, in short. Certainly, the waving of arms and branches is a way of warding off anxiety at the approach of dangerous animals; it may also serve the same purpose when a powerful chief or god approaches. The story of the palms laid in the path of Jesus on his arrival in Jerusalem is typical of many such incidents in which the waving of branches signifies dread. Burkert (1979:43ff.) argues that branches not only ward off a feared enemy, a god, or other worshipers but also can be offered or surrendered in gestures of welcome and sacrifice, a form of appeasement in which the people divest themselves of their weapons and appeal for help. Branches are extensions of the arms. The surrender of branches is not only a gesture of disarmament, a laying down of arms at the feet of the powerful figure who approaches. It is also a form of appeal. Thus surrendered, these branches may become a bed on which the powerful can rest (Burkert 1979:44). In any event, the surrender of such symbolic armaments is payment of respect, a tribute or dues paying; like the sacrifice of tithes, it wards off danger and averts a terrible disturbance. Therefore *dread expresses the combined emotions of fear and desire in a form of obligatory payment of dues, tribute, gifts, or sacrifice.*

The objects of such dread may be generic or quite specific. By "generic" I mean the universal and inevitable threats that face any society and every individual in the course of a generation. Each society faces enemies, invaders, dangerous strangers, and the threat of drought, plague, or famine. Similarly, each individual faces the generic enemies of the species: sickness and death, loss and betrayal, the envy and jealousy of friends and neighbors. Many of the threats to the community, however, are quite specific: *this* stranger, *this* plague. The corporate rites of thanksgiving over the plague that passed over the Hebrew people in Egypt are their response to a quite specific threat (and also may serve the purpose of preventing such disasters in the future). Finally, threats to an individual also may be quite specific; the rites engaged in by an individual may therefore not be intelligible to others, as in the case of the obsessive rites or idiosyncratic patterns observed by Freud. Burkert (1979:49–50) refuses to call these private rites "ritual" because they are not shared, but he also (1979:42) recognizes that an individual can make marks, like pouring oil on a stone, that later do become significant for others in the same or future generations, for example, Jacob's pouring of oil on a stone at Beth-el.

Conclusion

Fear and desire enter la vie serieuse *as an obligation to make a symbolic gesture of payment of unfulfilled societal or personal debt to generic or quite specific sources of help and danger.* Whether one includes individual gestures as religion depends on whether one wants to reserve the notion of religion or ritual for symbolic communications involving more than one or two persons. I have simply been concerned with establishing the notion of dread as a secularized form of the experience and expression of sin. As a secularized expression of the underlying emotions, dread is anxiety that something terrible will happen or that some opportunity will be missed unless a certain gesture is given and the underlying debt is paid.

Now, such dread in a secular society is more likely to be diffuse rather than concentrated. The payments can therefore be made at any time and any place rather than in a sanctuary set aside for the purpose of receiving such gifts. Indeed, Burkert (1979:52) argues that the concentration of such payments at holy places on holy occasions only came about with the evolution of social classes in antiquity. Prior to that *any* time and *any* place could occasion the payment of this debt. The development of a class of sanctuary priests who thus lived at the expense of the people required the privileged strata to offer protection against plague and predator, danger and disaster. Indeed, the failure of the king to ensure the fertility of the crops could be punishable with death, the punishment fitting the crime. The long, complex development of the obligations of the more privileged strata to protect the people arises from the initial payments of debt to ward off disaster. To put it simply: Dread creates a surplus of devotion, a treasury from which those who wish power can derive credit in return for offering the protection paid for by the particular offering.

Even modern systems that appear to be a "protection racket" or merely a mechanism of exchange depend on tapping the secularized treasury of psychological promises-to-pay. That was Durkheim's point. The more primitive effort to pay the debt owed to greed or to fate, to death or to nameless disaster, underlies the efforts of complex societies to face the specific and generic threats facing both the individual and the community. It remains to be seen whether complex systems can survive crises of motivation and commitment without seeking either priestly or bureaucratic means of inspiring dread. Certainly modern societies, like the most "primitive," have made it possible for dread to occur at any time or any place.

6

The Desire to Return
to the Source

───➤✝◄───

The diffuse sense of religious obligation has many
sources, of course. In the previous chapter we finished
by noting that the sense of obligation to the gods and to
heroes is expressed in sacrifices offered with heartfelt
thanksgiving for rescue from death. The desire for a safe
return from the foreign land of death, like the desire for
rescue, quickly becomes a sense of obligation to give
thanks and to sacrifice. The obligatory "sacrifice of
praise and thanksgiving" offered by Christians for nearly
two millennia is a case in point; the obligation directly
expresses a desire for rescue from death, and the thanksgiving is for the safe return of the dead to life: notably,
but not exclusively, the resurrected Jesus. Obligation is
based on the desire; when the desire is profound and
perennial, the resulting obligation appears to be abso-
lute and universal. Societies and communities differ in
whether the tribute to the Deity is to be paid in harmless
ritual, blood sacrifice, or the draft of young men for the
army. Eventually, the obligation to sacrifice becomes another source of danger from which the people must,
once again, be rescued. I propose that the way out of
this vicious circle is clearly to cut the cord linking desire to a sense of obligation, to cure the sense of sin by
forgiving psychological indebtedness.

The Desire to Recover One's Place

The sense of sin links another desire with a sense of religious obligation. That is the desire to recover sole access to one's original place in the universe. As Melanie Klein has reminded us, that place is the body of the mother (not just the womb). The desire to recover that space is symbolized in a baffling variety of ways. Thus one's place may be a home or a community, a place in an organization or an institution. One's place may be more general: a region, a countryside, or one's country, one's nation itself. One's place in the universe may also be symbolized in natural as well as social terms: a place of prominence, an island, a precipice or steeply descending slope. In the life of the imagination one's place has many forms, and social life draws much of its attraction and power from representing such a place to the unconscious as well as to the conscious mind.

In order to inspire dread, of course, the desire to return to the womb or to one's homeland must also inspire anxiety. The womb in retrospect can be an object of fear as well as of desire, a prison rather than a haven, a source of bondage rather than a desirable, unbreakable bond. In fact, the Daedalus myth begins with an expression of precisely this ambivalent desire for return combined with fear of being engulfed by the womb:

> Homesick for homeland, Daedalus hated Crete
> And his long exile there, but the sea held him.
> —Ovid 1955: Book VIII, ll. 183f.

Trapped by the sea and by the isolation of the island, Daedalus longed for home. In that longing to return, however, he began to feel trapped by the sea. I am arguing, however, that Daedalus was trapped by the wish to return home: the wish to be surrounded once again by the maternal embrace. It is the original maternal sea, the waters of the womb, that once held and—through his desire—hold him still.

The process of fusion, by which two separate units are made one, is also at the heart of any creative action. I have been pointing to the regressive tendency to seek reentry to the maternal womb and to fuse with the mother's body. The same process of putting together two objects or elements in such a way that a new one results that is different from the first two is fundamentally creative. Certainly this is how new molecules and compounds are made. It is also the way tools and materials are fashioned. In the realm of ideas, a new field emerges, for example, sociobiology, when the insights and methods of genetics and the social sciences are fused. I am speaking now of genuine creativity rather than tinkering or adaptation. To make something new is simply to make a new combination of elements in such a way that the constituent elements are indistinguishable and inseparable. That is innovation; indeed, the *daedaloi* were the innovators of antiquity. According to Ovid:

> He turned his thinking
> Toward unknown arts, changing the laws of nature.
>   —Ovid 1955: Book VIII, ll. 189–190

The same Daedalus who was creative was also the one homesick for his homeland and held by the sea. The way forward is inspired, then, by the energies that are directed backward to the mother. This was Freud's point about the similarity, in the long run, between the desires for satisfaction or pleasure and the desire for eternal rest or the Nirvana of the womb. The unpaid debt to the most profound desire is paid only when one is laid finally to rest; the satisfaction of that debt is, analytically speaking, the same as the satisfaction of the deepest longing for the mother.

The desire to recover one's original place in the world, the mother's body, can take on many forms. Disguised,

displaced, made relatively sublime or ridiculous, the desire knows any number of alternative lives in the mind.
Once transferred to the world of everyday social life, the
desire to return to the womb may become a desire for
sole occupancy of a place in someone's affections. The
same desire could turn into a concern for getting tenure:
the right to sole occupancy of one's place in an alma
mater. There are as many foster mothers offering such
space as there are organizations, for example, the offer of
exclusive occupancy of a desirable apartment or resort
accommodation. The appeal of such places is frequently
quite frank—the place is one's own, indefinitely, and it is
both nourishing and secure. Modern societies offer a
polymorphous, even perverse, variety of ways to satisfy
the desire for a return to the place of one's origin.

For such desires the world can offer no permanent or
complete satisfaction; that is why I speak of a surplus of
devotion. Such devotion, once the residue of unfulfilled
desire, becomes transformed into a serious obligation of
some sort. That obligation, of course, depends on the
context, that is, on whether one is trying to enjoy exclusive access to a territory or to a person, to a job or to a
set of ideas. The desire, translated into the world of the
intellect, becomes an insistence on one's viewpoint—a
desire to have the intellectual field to oneself rather than
to share the same intellectual space with others. If others' views are recognized, the recognition is only for the
sake of moving them to the periphery or eliminating
them entirely. The process of elimination can purify a
set of ideas from unwanted residues, from alternative
viewpoints, or from contaminating associations and
meanings. Purity is the goal of such elimination and can
become quite a serious intellectual obligation, since it
rests on such primitive mental foundations. Those foundations, Klein argued, are the infant's desire to take in
and to expel, to consume and to eliminate those who are
both loved and hated, especially the mother.

The infant is like a priest in its desire for purity, and like a criminal with imaginary ways of devouring and purging the self of those it wishes to consume and eliminate. In fact, it is the work of the thug to make sure that the community is purged of the presence of aliens and deviants. Stalin purged Russia of impure elements: bourgeois residues, small peasant landholders resisting collectivization, individuals who preferred to think for themselves. The most celebrated and disastrous purge for the sake of racial purity, the Jewish holocaust, transformed the nation into a thug, again in the service of the process of eliminating unwanted contaminants from the body politic. To the thug these are serious obligations, pursued with a devotion that is difficult to understand unless one assumes that the surplus of desire arises from the deepest psychic sources.

The scientific method also relies on the process of elimination to test its ideas. However inspired by intuitive or imaginative perceptions of the structure of chromosomes or the curvature of space, the ideas in question are pursued by eliminating alternative notions and hypotheses. One has to eliminate alternatives precisely in order to leave a notion intact. Scientific propositions are therefore no more authoritative than their most recent response to challenge; the last word is always waiting to be spoken. This apparent openness to challenge disguises the relentless search for purification inherent in the method: the insistence on eliminating alternative possibilities or sources of contamination. No purge of contrary hypotheses is ever complete, of course; it is a matter only of probabilities of which scientists can speak with certainty.

To this one might object that purity deserves a better name. Consider, for instance, the highly personal search for purification, especially when it focuses on specific ills or failings. Certainly Augustine's search for purity was at the time most damaging to himself, although his

African "wife" suffered from it, and so did his theological enemies. In the end, Augustine sought to purify his soul by examining himself with the words of the fifty-first psalm and spent his last days in penitential tears. Augustine's impediments were internal and spiritual, he believed, and only the most devoted self-purification through penitence could open for him the gates to paradise.

It is easy to discern the magical thinking that underlies attempts to purge the self of specific ills. The devotee's world, like the child's, is full of rivals, barriers, temptations, distractions—a wide range of impurities that prevent the earthly city from resembling or becoming the heavenly one. While one awaits the purging of the earthly city, one can operate on oneself. Instead of sticking needles into dolls in order to wound an adversary, one can, like Augustine, prick one's own soul and conscience in order to discern the point of painful self-awareness. It is at those points that the attempts to purify the self must concentrate.

In therapeutic attempts to uncover the more generic ills of depression and self-hatred, of course, one still concentrates on the specific ills of a patient's life, precisely because the patient seeks to avoid a direct approach to them. In the magical thinking of the child-turned-adult, however, these mental operations are intended to have a purgative effect. It is as if one could expel or eliminate the source of evil in the self and present the self unblemished, a pure and spotless sacrifice. Remember the discussion in chapter 5 of the patients described by Wallerstein, who needed to dramatize a basic fault (in Balint's sense of the term). Over and over again, they seemed driven to demonstrate that they were living a life of indebtedness at the expense of others. That is, they seemed to wish to mix their own resources with those of others, to borrow heavily from a world that stands ready to provide for them. The tendency was also obvious in the narcissistic patients who acted as if they felt entitled to unstinting support; "the Prince," for instance, enjoyed getting attention and being in demand, as though it were no less than his due (Wallerstein 1986:140). One woman with eating disturbances alternately deprived herself of food and stole from others. An obese woman who unconsciously still devoured her mother, chewing her to bits with a consuming hatred, she also engaged in shoplifting and ended up short-changing the analysis. Indeed, in her desire to maintain a direct, unmediated access to the world, as though to the mother's breast, she never resolved this fundamental fault of living in and through the eyes and affection of others. That is why eating was for her "both a gratification and a punishment" (Wallerstein 1986:290). In fact, she did not overcome her obesity during analysis (depriving herself and the analyst of the gratification that might come with such success), but the analyst also deprived her of such success by focusing more on her oedipal than on her pre-oedipal strivings, a form of collusion that may have protected the analyst from facing his feelings toward his own wife, who like the patient was both assertive and obese (Wallerstein 1986:293). The point is that the analyst embodies a social contract in which those who live at others' expense feel indebted and deprive themselves of real achievement. Outside the clinic those who pay what they experience as an unfair cost in a relationship end up by trying to make others pay. Social life may also be a way of colluding toward just such a mutual form of deprivation and indebtedness.

Unconscious aggressions underlie the feeling that a terrible debt must be paid either from others to oneself or by oneself to others. That is why, in the previous chapter, I discussed greed as a form of very aggressive, powerful drives to consume the environment and to make the world part of oneself. These are what are often called *destrudo:* a destructive drive akin to libido, which also is a primitive desire for life and satisfaction. Underlying this more demonstrative form of greed, however, is a passive greed, one that is often observed among patients who themselves seem very stubborn and dependent (Balint 1979:88). This drive for satisfaction is even more primitive, it seems, than the consuming passions of the infant, born of the mother, who seeks to cannibalize the world around it. What type of satisfaction is this?

Balint (1979) makes it very clear that there is a primary hunger that can only be understood as an expression of the infant's earliest relationship to its environment in the womb. In a number of passages he argues that the womb is indeed an environment, but it is also experienced as part of the infant. The distinction between inside and outside is real, since the infant experiences soft and flexible objects on the outside. That is why patients who have regressed to this stage demand flexibility and cushioning from their analysts (cf. Balint 1979:82ff.). Nonetheless, the relationship of what is outside to what is inside the infant is continuous, unbroken by sharp boundaries. After all, the water in the infant's lungs is indeed part of its environment. The exchanges with the environment are therefore smooth and harmonious. It is very difficult for an analyst to satisfy a patient's desire for this unbroken harmony, especially since the analyst maintains a certain distance by offering interpretations and by relying on speech, both techniques that violate the primitive harmony that the patient seeks to establish. Nonetheless, if analysts do not somehow satisfy this desire, patients may quite early on consign themselves to a relatively flat or even lifeless mode of existence (Balint 1979:88, 143). The point is that some forms of longing can only be satisfied at levels of the self where one imagines that one experiences full harmony with the world: the oceanic experience of which Freud spoke, or the presence of a Holy Spirit, as Paul put it, who is present when words fail (cf. Rom. 8:26). That is why the sin against the Spirit is unforgivable.

The Search for Primal Order

Fully to understand greed, then, we have to look beyond a desire to consume the world. There is a more primary satisfaction that is more like the Nirvana of vital existence, a profound and intense pleasure without striving (cf. Freud's essay *Beyond the Pleasure Principle*). There is a primal order that is sought here—the paradise in which one's thoughts and wishes are known before one speaks, and one exists distinctly and yet without separation from a world that responds with softness and flexibility to one's own movements. Attempts to restore that creation may therefore underlie the more obvious efforts to find remedies for sin: efforts to restore a world damaged by one's own greedy consumption. That is why the repetitive, seemingly childlike efforts of religious devotees to offer gifts to their gods—or of patients to give gifts to their analysts—so often fail to bring the desired satisfaction, which is a primary restoration that can only be achieved by a new creation (Balint 1979:127ff.).

The Protestant Reformation has given the individual the responsibility and powers of the priest to offer up a properly purified sacrifice to God. The task of self-purification therefore has become generalized from the sanctuary to the office or the kitchen. The modern individual accepts the obligation to purify the self, to engage in personal growth, and to fulfill his or her potential, which are the generic obligations of the modern self. Competitive strivings for exclusive access to some earthly paradise that is like the maternal body are mobilized for the process of self-improvement. The prize, however, remains a thinly disguised maternal milieu: a place where one's needs are met promptly without struggle or question. The pleasure principle, as Freud

reminded us, seeks the calm satisfaction of the womb,
the end of striving. That principle promises peace of
mind or soul; oriented toward self-improvement in the
competition for the rewards of social life, the pleasure
principle promises personal service—a "world" of satisfactions without challenge, interruption, or competition. Strivings cease in the matrix of the club or the
resort, the castle or the retirement community. The end
looks remarkably like the beginning: the grave and the
womb resemble each other, Freud insisted, and it becomes virtually impossible to distinguish the wish for
death from the desire for the womb. That is why eternal
life, in Christian thinking, often refers to both a victory
over death and an abundant source of life on earth. Sin is
quite literally no more.

The "priesthood of all believers" entitles each individual to make the operations necessary to save the
world and the self from emptiness and the grave. The
search for purity therefore has become a democratic
rather than an elite pursuit. In democratizing the pursuit
of purity, then, the West has tapped the enormous reserves of desire for earthly paradise, for the womb itself.
In tapping those reserves, Western societies also have
mobilized and sustained the obligations that had previously been monopolized by religion. Sacred obligations, the surplus of devotion once offered in sacrifice,
have been generalized to the entire population. There
they have become general obligations to vote, to work,
to improve the self, to purify the environment, to eliminate resistance and impediments to progress. As sin has
become secularized, so has the search for purification.

The residues of magical thinking are difficult to locate
when the purgatives have become routine and rational.
Nonetheless, there is a certain dread of not fulfilling the
serious obligation; for instance, individuals who publicly refuse to vote undergo various forms of shaming. It
is as if the pulling of a lever were a means of offering a

sacrifice, a form of civic tribute; its operations are intended to ensure certain effects in the world, although there is widespread doubt and even cynicism about whether the effects achieved are the ones intended. Votive offerings in ritual are quite simple and direct in their operation; an idol thrown on the fire represents the one whose impurities of soul or body are being purged. The collective offering of these small representations could purify an entire community of its ills and ensure both public and private well-being for the coming year. In such rites magical thinking is clear and obvious. This magical thinking is latent in the collective rites of purification that occur in Western democracies on their occasions of periodic renewal.

Consider the passions aroused when blacks demonstrated during the 1960s for their right to vote and to take their place at the public table. The mobilization of white civil rights workers in the South focused on the demand that blacks be able to make their offerings at the altar of civic responsibility: their right to vote. The exhumation of the bodies of the three workers buried in Mississippi confirmed that no sacrifice was too great in such a cause. The generic obligation to vote can thus be a form of collective self-purification. Whether the right to vote, when exercised, can affect the material fortunes of the black population is currently in doubt; it was made an issue in the presidential campaign of Jesse Jackson. Residues of magical thinking lead to the insistence that the manual operations of the voting machine produce the desired effects on the body politic. That possibility remains to be realized. In the meantime, the fervor of political mobilization suggests that there are deep wells of devotion from which the nation can still draw its measure of political credits.

Think of the surplus of devotion as a treasury of merit from which a society can acquire credit. That credit is extended to those who represent the fulfillment of the desire for a greater peace and prosperity: the end of strivings and the guarantee of nourishment and safety. Tapping that desire in the form of devotion is the task of priests and politicians; it is the job of educators and scientists. The reservoir of devotion can also be a source of credit for industries that promise to cure illness, remove pollutants from the atmosphere, and defend the nation's borders from danger and invasion. The task is twofold: to transform the desire for earthly paradise into civic obligation and to associate that obligation with the performance of certain operations—voting, study, self-improvement, attendance at school, attention to politicians, proper diet and exercise, and the recitation of such formulas as the Pledge of Allegiance, one's rights at the moment of being arrested, and the oath to tell nothing but the whole truth.

In magical thinking, the individual attempts to change the world by engaging in some operation, for example, by carving, burning, or sticking pins into some effigy or by performing various operations on the self. Some individuals seek to eliminate rivals by purging the self of their representations in the mind and body. No wonder members of hostile groups avoid one another. One dreads the sight of a rival whom one has unconsciously eliminated. The rival, as Rank reminded us, can also be a double of the self.

The self models the world that it seeks to possess, change, consume, or destroy. Even the body becomes the representative of the space that the person seeks to occupy—in this case, the womb itself. As Klein argued, the child purges the womb of rivals by eliminating any internal impurities that might get in the way—that is, internalized objects of hatred. Children often seek to turn their anger toward a rival into a bit of waste matter, and the feces then become representatives of the hated rival. To eliminate the rival by evacuating the bowels becomes a magical operation on the world, performed, however, on the individual's own body. That is how magic works, only in this case the votive offering is a part of one's own body.

Some sociologists have criticized various forms of self-improvement among adults as child's play. When the purpose behind consciousness-raising or self-improvement is to make the world into a better place, residues of magical thinking may well be hard at work. The logic goes: If only I become aware of sexism or racism in the larger society, that awareness will bring an increased immunity from the disease or an ability to root out its sources. Awareness, as blacks and women increasingly attest, does raise consciousness but does not necessarily have any effect on the larger society. It may simply add the insult of conscious victimization to the injury of being discriminated against.

In a society that begins to doubt its own means of self-purification, demands for purity may take an ugly turn. When education and voting, hard work and the cultivation of the correct attitudes, fail to improve the material conditions of the middle class, people can demand more strenuous forms of purification. Get rid of pornography. Stop abortions. Better yet: Remove gays, secular humanism, illegal immigrants; remove from the schools children who refuse to recite the Pledge of Allegiance. Keep drugs out of the country, along with such other foreign intrusions as imported cars, capital, and ideas. Stop acid rain. Shut down nuclear reactors. Clear up the rivers and bays.

Demand for purity of the larger society becomes more intense and becomes fixed on quite specific sources of impurity and pollution when generic obligations, for example, work and education, voting and oath taking, fail to purify the society, to make it safe and clean, and to improve the lot of its devotees. The surplus of devotion is not an inexhaustible source of social credit. When it reaches a dangerously low level, the devoted begin to

demand effective ways of eliminating very specific impurities from the body politic.

Some of the demands for purification listed above
came from the left, others from the right. What matters is
not whether one is engaged in the politics of purification on the side of the liberals or conservatives. It is the
same politics, however different may be the specific
sources of impurity targeted for elimination. What
passes for critical political commentary amounts to a series of positions taken on each issue. What about gays?
What about abortion? What about the environment? The
reduction of the demand for purity to specific issues is
partly the result of living in a complex society.

Such reductionism is also the result of a regression in
critical thinking: a step backward in the ability of a society to diagnose and cure its own ills. To turn problematic emotions and relationships into specific ills, like a
pain in the abdomen or a headache, is the result of hys-
teria in the individual. *Such political reductionism is
equally hysterical, no matter how clear and lucid,
rational and technical, are the discussions in the apparently inexhaustible publications and policy statements of religious and secular institutions.*

Demands for purity escalate, then, when the supply of
surplus devotion is beginning to run dry. When there is
no reservoir of public credit on which politicians can
run for office, the search for flaws becomes very intense.
Did the candidate plagiarize in college or in his political
speech-making? Did the candidate avoid service in the
armed forces or earn a mediocre record in college? Has
the candidate falsified his or her report of behind-the-
scenes negotiations while in office? When the surplus of
devotion runs low, the electorate puts its leaders on a
very short leash indeed. To take them at their word is no
longer possible. What matters are the facts underlying
the claims, the results rather than the promises. What
seems like the reduction of public debate to the issue of

character is actually the deflation of the supply of credit in the political system and in the society at large. The coin of public trust is in short supply.

The same reduction in the surplus of devotion makes individuals skeptical of the long-term benefits of their own sacrifices, efforts, and commitments. It is not only the larger society that is running on empty; it is the individual who doubts that hard work in school will pay off in fruitful and dignified work. The same fragile tie that allows individuals to invest themselves in a vocation or, somewhat less ambiguously and for a shorter term, to lend themselves to a career is broken; in its place is an outright demand to make money, plenty of it, in as short a time as possible.

The rituals of education, of voting, of attention to public affairs, allow individuals to lend their moral and intellectual energies, as well as their time and often their money, to the public sphere. When these rites fail, the reservoir of public obligation reaches a dangerously low level. The young do not attend the rites of the community; if they do, they hold themselves back rather than give of themselves wholeheartedly. It is too late, at such times, for a candidate to warn the young against asking what their country can do for them; that is indeed what they are asking. To encourage them to ask what they can do for their country is like banking on a thrift whose reservoirs are sorely depleted.

Even in a modern society it is dangerous when the young disregard the rites in which they are intended to lend themselves to the community and to the nation. Lack of attendance in public schools poses a danger to the survival of the society. The emphasis during the election of 1988 on the Pledge of Allegiance or on prayer in the schools is simply another symptom of justifiable public anxiety that the young are not giving themselves to the larger society; they are not replenishing the reservoirs of obligation. When the surplus has been drained, the public becomes impatient and throws objects on the playing field. Gangs of youths run through the arena, robbing the audience. Attendance at churches runs low, except where congregations have found ways to keep the young involved; there the growth of the churches comes from a new supply of younger members, while other denominations languish. It is these growing churches, often the evangelical, that have shown a new interest in national politics, new zeal for public policy-making, and increasing numbers of members both registered to vote and voting. The question is whether their contributions can create a surplus of devotion among those who have typically transformed a wide range of desires into duties. *The point is that these churches are the most vocal in proclaiming the notion that humankind suffers from a primal flaw: an original sin.*

7

Scapegoating the Individual

————→✠←————

Any individual is clearly a source of danger to society's ability to reproduce itself. As late as the Middle Ages, Coleman (1982) argues, the individual's place in the entire social system depended on his or her place in the family, that is, in the social unit closest to nature itself. Not all members of a family household, of course, were kin; many were servants, slaves, or serfs. Not all the kin, furthermore, had the rights and responsibilities of a person in modern societies; on the contrary, it is only recently that women have been accorded the rights of citizenship and the responsibilities of making contracts. In the Middle Ages only male owners and their heirs, usually the eldest son, had the prerogatives and responsibilities of personhood, and these came by virtue of their place in the system, with responsibilities delegated from above and exercised over those below. These responsibilities inhered not in the individuals but in their positions within the household. The household in turn consisted not of positions so much as statuses for persons: the young and the old, the men and the women, the slave and the free. The corporate actor of that older order was the family, and the structure of the society was built on that institution. The state, the church, even the commerce of that period were extensions of the family. It was relatively easy, under such conditions, to make the larger society the object of sacred obligation and to restrain individualism.

The Corporate Actor

That order has changed, Coleman writes, with the introduction of a new corporate actor very much different from the family. Coleman writes:

> The new corporate actor from which much of modern social and economic structure is composed is founded on different assumptions than the family. It is a structure of activities, not of persons, with positions or offices as nodes of the structure. A person is born into a family; membership in it is what some sociologists call ascribed, while membership in modern corporate actors is, by this same terminology, achieved, that is, a result of voluntary choice on the part of the person or the corporate actor or both. (1982:124)

Anyone familiar with basic sociological ideas will realize that there is little new here except the emphasis on a new breed of corporate actors: not individuals who personify corporate actors, like the family, but corporate actors per se. The larger society, and the state in particular, becomes an impersonal structure.

The distinguishing characteristic of this new species is limited liability. The individuals who are employed do not make up the corporate actor, no matter how often their pictures appear in the brochures of the company and no matter how often the company speaks of itself as a family. What makes up the company is not individuals-in-statuses but positions. Empty the positions of their incumbents and put new ones in their places, and it is the same company. Try that with the family. Replace all members in their several statuses with new individuals, and— presto—you have a different family. It is really as simple as that. The new corporate actor has a life of its own. The state goes on, regardless of who holds office. Authority is wholly impersonal. Under these conditions, to complain of "individualism as a besetting social sin" is to blame the victim. It is the individual who has become extraneous.

In Coleman's view, the old form of corporate actor, the family as an institution, made every adult both a warden and a ward—a warden with responsibilities for certain others in his or her care and with corresponding authority over them, and yet also a ward of those of higher status or estate. As wardens they saw to it that the crops were sown and harvested, that the children were trained or educated, that whatever capital could be raised from the sale of homespun or candles, for instance, or of other products of the household was stored for the purchase, perhaps, of another acre. There was capital, but it was raised from the continued work of the whole family. Liability was total, and the lives of each depended on the work of all. *The modern corporate actor may not ask or receive less work from the individuals it employs, but it nevertheless takes far less responsibility for their care.* The person as such becomes a "temp," although individuals may stay employed by the same company for years. The *system* separates from the persons within it.

The old order has not gone completely, but it is going, and the emerging order, such as it is, that comes from the new breed of corporate actors has not yet filled all the vacancies of care and control. Here is how Coleman puts it:

> As the old social structure receded into history (most rapidly in the last half century), it left a vacuum of responsibility. *For when authority was no longer over the person but only over those activities carried out in the time given to the corporate actor, responsibility contracted as well.* When the individual left the hierarchy of the old structure and entered the market of the new one, he left the protection of the patron and found no other protection fully to replace it. (1982:125, emphasis added)

A circular process therefore begins to foster a type of emigration from the larger society. The less protection, recognition, or support one receives from institutions or the larger society, the more one invests in one's own immediate, microsocial world without regard to official sanctions or support. The larger society becomes increasingly less compelling, trustworthy, rewarding, interesting, or necessary as a condition for getting on with one's life. The nation is perceived to be secular to the extent that individuals withdraw from it their contributions of money and time, energy and trust, loyalty and obedience. This withdrawal of emotional commitment may very well leave the individual feeling guilty. Certainly, the nation becomes far less the object of devotion, it becomes far less sacred as a national community and more recognizably secular. The nation may be shortchanged.

Some individuals may not feel guilty for shortchanging the country. Take, for example, the payment of taxes to the nation. In testimony before Congress, two New York City reporters described in some detail their observations of New Yorkers who were operating in cash so as to avoid reporting income and paying taxes on it. For many, it was "natural," a "way of life," a matter of their "survival," according to these reporters (U.S. Congress 1979). Cabbies, waitresses, street sales people, wholesalers, domestics—all had adopted the strategy of receiving their pay or making their sales in cash so as to avoid reporting their income. Others were far more secure: doctors, lawyers, and professionals who kept two sets of books, one for themselves and one for the IRS (U.S. Congress 1979:273). Both those paying in cash and those receiving in cash "felt no guilt," said one reporter, a Mr. Moritz; the other reporter, a Ms. Kramer, made the same point:

> And other professional people I spoke to just felt that was part of the game, of the income tax game, that if you have a way of not reporting all of your taxes, that you were almost obligated to find a way. I mean it is just like tax shelters have become a way of life in upper-income families. And I

think that finding some way of not reporting your income is kind of a way of life for a lot of professional people. They do it. And they think it legal. They do not worry about it not being legal. (U.S. Congress 1979:270–271)

There is nothing permanent about a cash transaction, just as there is little that can be taken for granted in a cash economy. As Marx reminded us, the ties that bind us in the cash nexus are temporary and perishable. That is why it is possible to speak of taxation as a game rather than as a sacred duty.

Later in the same hearing there was some disagreement between the reporters on whether the better educated, the professionals, were apprehensive of being discovered cheating on their taxes. One congressman made the point, however, that the underlying issue is that individuals will cheat on taxes or on other forms of obligation to the state, like the draft, *when they feel that their government has cheated on them.* The sense of being shortchanged may well be one cause of the tendency to under-withhold taxes; I will return to that possibility later. It is clear, however, that these reporters had found widespread practices and attitudes that indicated that many individuals from a variety of social classes feel little compunction about avoiding taxes. I am suggesting that they might have a stronger predisposition to pay their taxes if they felt that they occupied a permanent and guaranteed status rather than a temporary position that rests on their achievement alone. There was nothing sacred about their obligation to pay tribute.

To secede from modern societies by withholding taxes, however, does not require the permission of the clergy or ritual celebration, even if one engages in a tax revolt based on one's religious conscience. Of course, the feeling that one shares a common fate with other members of the nation can lead to voluntary compliance with tax law, particularly in wartime. Even in wartime, however, there are many who find the ways and means to avoid payments to the national treasury and other forms of self-sacrifice. As one commentator on national sentiments in England during World War II has put it,

> Despite the common danger and the common loyalties [the war] was expected to engender, evasion of rationing, etc., was always thought to be unpatriotic but was often the subject of banter or even social boasting by normally law-abiding citizens as well as by habitual black-marketeers. (Seldon 1979:4)

Under these conditions, the connection between individual and national survival could hardly be clearer, and yet evasion of the law was widely tolerated. We can only speculate on the unconscious guilt incurred by living in wartime quite literally at others' expense.

In peacetime, however, the act of avoiding taxes signifies that the citizen is minimally committed to the larger society: a "temp," as it were. Tax avoidance then becomes less an act of rebellious departure than a symptom of the way the society as a whole treats the person. It might well be, as Arthur Seldon went on to argue, that "money is being asked for by government for services that it does not have to supply, and that it supplies them less satisfactorily than they could be supplied in the market" (Seldon 1979:14). Although the reference here is primarily to England, the argument applies equally to the United States, where the under-reporting of income has frequently been considered a form of "tax-revolt" against a government that is not only too big but also wasteful and occasionally corrupt in awarding contracts and monitoring expenses. So, far from being rebels or émigrés, these individuals are reminding the government to avoid unnecessary services and curtail fraud and waste—a reminder that was taken seriously by the House subcommittee from whose hearings I have quoted testimony. When the citizen becomes a "temp" like the employee, it adds insult to injury for the government to squander its tax revenues. A person whose contributions to the sacrificial system are increasingly minimal and temporary will not gladly tolerate corruption or waste.

Even in modern societies, however, there are residues of guilt. The sacrificial system operates through the labyrinth of the state. Some religious groups are more likely than others to consider paying taxes a moral, if not a sacred, duty. Consider these figures on tax evasion or protest against taxes in several European countries. Bracewell-Milnes (1979:78–79) notes a wide difference between a country that is largely Protestant in heritage, such as Norway, and a country that is predominantly Catholic, such as Italy. In Norway about 5 to 15 percent of taxes on income is *evaded,* whereas in Italy one study estimates that only 10 percent of taxes (other than those collected "at the source") is actually *collected.* Other data, from Holland, also suggest that Protestant-Catholic differences do affect the taxpayer's sense of obligation to the larger society, among individuals with clear political affiliations. One study of Holland notes, for instance, that in 1975 about 39 percent of adult men and women questioned in a national poll agreed either that it is "all right to leave part [of taxable income] unreported" or that the taxpayer should "try to pay no tax at all" (Bracewell-Milnes 1979:73), and on this point there were no major differences among Protestants and Catholics. Such differences do emerge, however, in connection with political affiliation. Only 28 percent of those reporting that they had voted for either of two Protestant parties (the Anti-Revolutionary or Christian Historical) were willing to condone tax evasion, but 44 percent of those voting for the Catholic party (KVP) were willing to do so. It appears that once they become politicized, Protestants are more likely than Catholics to consider taxation a legitimate form of sacrifice to the larger society. Perhaps that is because Catholics may be more willing than Protestants to restrict their loyalties to the world of face-to-face relationships and to the religious community itself.

There is, moreover, an increasing vacuum of responsibility in a society whose actors are increasingly corporate. On one front page of the *Wall Street Journal* (Feb. 2, 1987) there were two stories about the failure of contractual obligations. An article in the far left-hand column reported on bankruptcies and bank failures during recent economic "good times." The rate resembled what one would expect during a recession. The point of the article was simple enough: that bad times in the future could make the current rate of such disasters seem relatively mild. In the right-hand column on the same page an article described in tragic detail the failure of many medical labs to provide reliable results of clinical tests. One woman, whose Pap tests had been consistently negative, found out too late that she had cancer; her body was by then saturated with it. A marriage broke up when one partner received a positive result from a syphilis test; the test was simply in error, but the error was not confirmed in time to save the marriage. The point of these stories was simple enough: Contracts with labs to provide reliable test results in return for fees are not enforced, may not be enforceable under current law, and leave individuals vulnerable to unnecessary suffering and even mortal danger. Both articles provided tragic documentation of a vacuum of corporate responsibility and default on contracts. If irresponsible "individualism" characterizes corporate actors like banks and laboratories, why blame their victims—mere persons?

There is simply no doubt that contracts are going by the boards, whether because interest rates drive farmers out of business, changing oil prices cripple businesses and the banks that have lent them money, or carelessness and greed make it possible for laboratories to ruin lives. To put it in the more formal terminology of the sociologist, macrosocial trends are intruding into the microsocial sphere. Everyday life provides no safety from distant social trends. Those trends are more than economic (affecting interest rates or oil prices, for example); they are certainly not merely legal (affecting the regulations of labs). Sociologists since Durkheim have noted that contracts rest on a far more tenuous basis even than the law and the economy; they rest on unstated assumptions, moral commitments, and implicit agreements, without which they are not valid. *It is not merely the reliability of contracts that makes everyday life possible; it is their validity.* Without a firm base in the unspoken premises of a whole society, contracts will be very weak and unreliable supports even in good times. When such contracts lose their binding power, for whatever reason, the sacrificial system itself becomes highly visible. When the Minotaur is clearly the government or banking system, there is no abiding reason for either tribute or sacrifice. The Protestant miracle is that so many are still willing to make their sacrifices to the larger society.

The Vacuum of Responsibility

If the United States were small, homogeneous, or simple enough to be a moral community, it would make sense for politicians, preachers, and sociologists to join together in a campaign for the moral rearmament of America. Indeed, there are persistent political voices calling for all Americans to bear the burdens of a few, for residents of one region that prospers to uphold the residents of another region who have suffered adversity, and for America to put into political practice the moral virtues of the family, where positions are for life rather than for the time being. There are preachers who claim with some justification that private virtues can do the public some good, and that the public sphere should inculcate private virtues. There are also some sociologists who are issuing similar calls to Americans to remember that they are a community, or at least to remember that they have been one in times past and can be one again if they find a language commensurate with their faith. Each of these voices seeks to justify the sacrificial system and to ensure a continuous supply of fresh sacrifices. Each seeks to make the fate of the larger society the common destiny of every individual and to scapegoat "individualism." All argue that Americans together share a common fate; it is up to each one of us to realize and to shape it for the benefit of all. If they speak of sin, it is to reinforce a sense of permanent obligation rather than to point to a way out. There will be no forgiveness of debt for the American citizen.

Americans are not alone in failing to perceive that their individual destinies may well depend on their nation's fate. Cantril (1965) once supervised a study called "The Pattern of Human Concerns" and found that Americans were unlikely to link their personal sense of optimism or pessimism with their outlook for the nation. The correlation between their sense of their own future and their estimate of their nation's future was relatively low. In this respect they resembled the citizens of such large, amorphous, and relatively less industrialized countries as Mexico and India. Similar studies of Americans in the 1970s found that, for several years in a row, Americans responded with increasing pessimism about the future of their country; in the same period they responded with increasing optimism about their own personal futures (American Institute of Public Opinion, in Watts and Free 1978:tables 1–1, 1–7). The awareness of a common fate was indeed decreasing. I am arguing that the "times" of the nation and the "times" of the individual are out of joint. Under these conditions it may well be possible to point the way toward canceling the unnecessary debt of the individual toward a larger society that does not respect mere persons as such. This divorce between an individual's view of the nation's prospects and that individual's view of his or her own future is another reason for a declining sense of obligation to the larger society. It makes plausible the increasing tendency to keep one's transactions secret by failing to report all one's income. The process reflects a decline in the numbers of those who feel that the nation itself can provide one a living, or security, or a piece of the public pie. This diminished sense of a nation's contribution to the individual may be a reason for the individual's own withdrawal of tribute. If the relation of the person to the nation is not only minimal, for the time being, but also part of a quite different time "zone," there is no way for the nation to legitimate the call to sacrifice.

Nonetheless, the churches have tried to keep alive the emotional residues of earlier sacrificial systems and to perpetuate their obligation to the point of new sacrifices. Take, for example, the notion of the church as a household of faith. That idea is based on premodern conditions in which the household itself, an extension of the family, ordered all relationships in a hierarchy of statuses. The core of that hierarchy was, of course, the patriarchal line linking father to eldest son in rights of inheritance and succession—the core of the Daedalus complex itself. That same line figures prominently in Christian theology; there a divine father and divine-human son provide the core of an order that extends throughout the household of God into the world. That world is linked by ties not of kinship but of faith, and its relations extend, in the Western city, beyond those of the same religion to those who inhabit the same territory, the earthly city. On the relation of this heavenly order to an earthly city, much Christian theology has attempted to elaborate. The point, however, is that the metaphor of a household that extends through ties to those in "the world" has provided one way of extending the sacrificial system to the larger society. The church still sees itself positioned in the world as a household, rooted in a divine family, extended by a network of obligations through a variety of servants and coworkers into a larger theater of political, legal, and commercial relations. The status of a person in that theologically conceived community is given by rites of sacrificial initiation. As Coleman pointed out, it is a status ascribed, in the traditional sense, rather than achieved. With it comes the open, diffuse, and lifelong set of obligations that underwrite the rights of citizenship in the larger society.

It is easier to find the relevance of this conception of obligation to the rural society of the Middle Ages than it is to find its relevance to a complex urban social system in the twentieth century. As the Daedalus complex reveals, moreover, the roots of this conception are not uniquely Christian; they extend into antiquity. Indeed, Christianity learned much of this from the Roman order, whose civic and military regimes were equally patriarchal and familial. In each the household was the basis of social order. In it the heirs and the servants found their place, their respective statuses, in an order of obligation and obedience that extended from the most divine to the most lowly human.

To preempt this old order, to nullify its obligations and neutralize its remaining appeal, the churches necessarily had to pronounce that old order "finished." That is what it means to secularize the authority of a social system—to consign it to a period or epoch that is passing away. To abandon such a system requires a decisive act of withdrawal from it, an act in which the person emerges from the protections and confinements of a status in the system or abandons all hope for such status. That is why Christianity is credited with being a revolution of the person and therefore profoundly individualistic. It offers a way to secularize social time by personal choice rather than by the cataclysm of the ancient regime.

In complex societies religion no longer has the ability to fill the "vacuum of responsibility." It is a real vacuum, but it is left to other professions to fill it. The medical profession, which has power to fill the vacuum, resists doing so. While doctors hold out the promise of a brighter future through medical technology and practice, they pass on a disproportionate share of the costs of that dream to their clients. Andrew Stein noted as president of the New York City Council:

> It is virtually unheard of for a doctor to be prosecuted, even when patients die as a consequence of gross negligence. Doctors also seem immune to any serious professional discipline. There are surely more than 20,000 grossly incompetent physicians nationwide [the figure of 20,000 being the estimate of the editor of the *New England Journal of Medicine*], yet the licenses of only 260 doctors were revoked in 1984. (*New York Times,* Feb. 2, 1986: Op-Ed page)

Mr. Stein goes on to note that the vast majority of licenses were revoked not for medical incompetence but for other abuses, such as fraud; furthermore, the vast majority of cases are reported not by the medical profession but by others, including their victimized clients. Required by law to report "medical misconduct," doctors simply fail to do so; no wonder Mr. Stein goes on to argue that "the suffering caused by negligent practice in this country and in the state is simply unacceptable—and the failure to crack down on incompetent doctors constitutes a scandal" (ibid.). The key terms here are "unacceptable" and "a scandal." Such a vacuum of responsibility is no longer filled by appeals to a once-sacred doctor-patient relationship. That shrine is now empty. It is, therefore, not surprising that the sacrifices of the citizen to the medical profession and the health care system are now coming under close inspection. The question is whether the public reservoir of obligation has dropped to a level so low that no one will be able to mobilize rational support for sustaining the health care system.

Earlier societies had to manage the dynamic individual will that inspired prophetic utterance, initiated capitalist ventures, and demanded to be tested in a wide range of conflicts. Modern societies, however, have been more successful in taming the individual will and in putting it to official use. When the will is a matter of routine, work goes on at a regular, if unexciting, pace. The demand for testing is satisfied by accountants who can assess returns on investments, by scientists who can vouch for the results of experiments, or by managers who can get results. At its absurd extreme, rationalization leads to such rigorous and minute testing as determinations of quarterly returns on investment or—a more tragic example—body counts in a distant war. The spirit becomes lost in its service to industrial, bureaucratic, military, or civic goals. A disenchanted social system therefore has pervasive effects on everyday life, but it is also neither immediately relevant to the individual nor an object of moral commitment. The separation between the sources of inspiration of the individual and the routines of the office measures the distance between personal values and corporate goals and processes.

Some sociologists have been highly disapproving of this pulling apart. They find in it the seeds of disintegration: individualism, the loss of the sacred, and the erosion of values that guarantee the social contract. Durkheim is perhaps the most celebrated sociologist to argue that particular contracts are the outward and visible sign of an inward and spiritual set of values and commitments. Contracts are indeed the flesh and bones of a society. Banks must keep enough money on hand to "redeem" their obligations, just as farmers must pay their debts. Laboratories must provide reliable results if they are not going to endanger life itself. But this reliability in living up to the terms of a contract depends in part on the spiritual core of a society, that is, on what Durkheim called collective sentiments. In their absence, contracts are nothing more than flesh and bone unnourished by values and beliefs. Under these conditions, some individuals quietly go about their corporate business in a pragmatic or utilitarian fashion, indifferent to the public consequences of their actions. Durkheim was extremely critical of pragmatism and utilitarianism that were not based on more profound commitments. In the United States, such individualists as Nixon, North, and Boesky are known to operate within the protection of corporate actors—the state; Kidder Peabody; Goldman Sacks; Morgan Stanley; or Drexel Burnham. It is this individualism of corporate actors that constitutes the disintegration of the larger society. Under these conditions, there is no hope for the mere person as such, but there is also no reason for the sacrificial system to go unchallenged. The Minotaur is all too visible at the center of the labyrinth. Why, then, should the churches seek to keep alive the residues of the sacrificial system at all?

The new breed of corporate actors has the legal rights and responsibilities of the individual; their liabilities, however, may be limited to the original investment of the partners. Similarly, their authority may be equally limited by the time and energy invested by their agents and employees. Some companies take limited responsibility for the health and welfare of their employees, and even less for their employees' spiritual development or for child care. Granted that there may be an extension of corporate programs in each of these areas; there may not, however, be a major extension of corporate responsibilities. *That is precisely the point: that with an au-*

*thority circumscribed by the formal purpose of a
company (i.e., to make a profit or produce educational materials), the company's responsibilities will
be similarly circumscribed. This new breed of corporate actors, some economic and others political, some
profitable and others clearly not profitable, extrudes
the person and is responsible for the spread of "corporate individualism."* This leaves the individual as *person* a mere survivor of the labyrinth.

8

The Daedalus Complex
and the Churches

For several years the courts in the United States have been witnessing an increase in litigation with a heightening demand for compensations for what individuals have suffered—that is, a demand for a settling of accounts. There is, no doubt, a complex set of factors contributing to this increased litigation; I do not intend either to oversimplify or to deal here with this problem as such. However, this litigiousness itself indicates a heightened awareness of unsatisfied desires and a growing refusal to answer the call to sacrifice. To dismiss this litigiousness as another indication of individualism, however, is to miss the depth of its motivation and to trivialize its seriousness. To label it pejoratively as individualism is also to scapegoat individuals for a greed that is deeply institutionalized in American social life, including in the churches themselves.

The courts, after all, are like many churches. To the courtroom individuals come to plead their own cases, to hear the law read to them, to listen to testimony, to make confession, to stand before the bar of at least penultimate justice, and to avoid the final test of wills and strength that occurs when the courts—like the churches—fail in their liturgical tasks. That so many individuals want to have their day in court instead of making unnecessary sacrifices or fulfilling some unspoken sense of public duty is evidence that the Daedalus complex is still widespread and unresolved. The place where individuals go to seek relief, however, is the courtroom rather than the sanctuary. Now the judicial system, supported by panels of specialists in ethics, psychology, and the social sciences, defines the delicate balance between duty and desire.

Ever since Durkheim wrote his well-known, however flawed, study of suicide, sociologists have tried to understand the devastating consequences of an imbalance between desire and duty. A relative preponderance of unsatisfied desire, of desire not transformed into duty, may result in what Durkheim called egoistic or anomic suicide. Like Icarus, individuals can self-destruct when the limits on their ambitions seem suddenly to disappear. Conversely, an individual overwhelmed by duty and the subordination of desire may engage in what Durkheim called altruistic or fatalistic suicide. Like Daedalus, the individual sacrifices the self and its desires to some arbiter of human freedom and destiny, be it divine or human: Apollo or the state.

From a Durkheimian sociological perspective, society is indeed the final arbiter, just as it is the source, of all freedom and of individual identity. The desires in question are various. They range from a wish to own and control the sources of our lives to a desire to pay back those at whose expense we feel ourselves to have been living. Those desires may be directed toward the living or the dead, toward others or toward ourselves. They may be positive, in the sense of seeking new unities, or negative, in the sense of removing all obstacles to our satisfaction. Under the impact of repression, however, these desires are transmuted into a vague and diffuse sense of obligation: of unfinished action, of appointments not kept, of payments not made, of tribute or even sacrifice withheld. It is this compound of desire repressed and sublimated into duty, with its predisposition to sacrifice, that I have been calling the Daedalus complex.

When the Church Compounds Guilt

If there is a single institution that has been expert at mobilizing this diffuse sense of emotional indebtedness, it is the church. For instance, the desire of individuals to settle their accounts with the dead or to achieve new forms of communion with their parents can be easily transformed into a set of ecclesiastical duties and obligations. Devotion becomes a duty to serve at the altar, to take Communion, to sing in the choir, to utter the prayers, and to preserve the faith of one's first family. The desire to settle accounts with those who have hurt or offended one can quickly be transformed into a keen sense of social justice or into more apocalyptic urges for restitution and even revenge.

The failure of the individual to grow and develop, to achieve new mastery and control, and to satisfy some basic desires for contentment and release can be transformed under the impact of any religious institution into an obligation to fulfill one's true vocation, to find oneself under the auspices of the church, and to offer one's entire life as a debt to be paid only when life itself is relinquished. These are heavy duties, and the church historically has been expert in imposing them on clergy and laity alike, despite its gospel of the forgiveness of debts.

In the tensions created by this complex of debts and desires, the clergy are often set at odds with the laity, especially where calls to sacrifice are concerned. The clergy's appeals to do justice to those who have been injured, ignored, or excluded by the larger society touch the laity's sense of unfulfilled desire and unpaid debt to themselves and to others: on the point of their vulnerability, as it were. If it were the laity's compassion that were being touched by the clergy's exhortations, rather than their sense of emotional indebtedness, perhaps the

laity would not take such offense at the clergy's prophetic stance on various social issues.

Of course, there are other interests that might put the
laity at odds with a liberal social position. I am speaking,
however, of the intensity of the laity's reaction to the
churches' frequent reminders that the laity have a social
duty to perform and that they may even be called upon
to make further sacrifices. Are the laity becoming disenchanted with a church that, while promising relief from
this complex of dutiful and sacrificial motives, in fact
intensifies and exploits them?

The question itself may seem offensive and calls for
some interpretation. Perhaps an example will help. Consider, for instance, George Will's diatribe against the liberal tendencies that have sought to redress the injuries
inflicted on minority groups and third world countries
by prosperous classes and nations. I quote Will despite
the fact that his resentment is informed by a conservative
political stance that I do not endorse. It is his sense of
being aggrieved over perennial reminders of obligation
that is useful here. Listen to the tone of these remarks; I
find in them the tenor of many comments made by the
laity to their parish clergy over the last thirty years of
social change. Demands especially for reparations for
"historic injustices," he writes, "dominate political
agendas; they are psychological taxes levied by professional victims against non-victims who have inherited
guilt. Politics . . . becomes a melodrama about the redemption of a sinful society, particularly the middle
class" ("The Journey Up from Guilt," George Will,
Newsweek, June 25, 1990:4). To what extent, then, has
the church become a school for professional victims?

What Will calls "the politics of guilt" turns compassion into duty and sours, therefore, the wells of genuine
social justice. The society is blamed, rather than the individual, for social ills; the welfare state prospers ac-
cordingly, and individual offenders are allowed to go

free. The recent shift to a more conservative political climate, he argues, is due to the growing realization that individuals are responsible for their actions; hence the growing refusal to take on oneself the burden of payments for others' crimes. Here, then, is a journalist entering the public debate about the imbalance between desire and duty that results in unnecessary sacrifices.

As Will's example indicates, the arbiters of the transformation of desire into duty now include many other professions besides the clergy; the *daedaloi* are now called by a variety of names—journalists like Will, therapists, psychoanalysts, educators, and social workers, to name a few. The knowledge of guilt that has been lost to the more pragmatic and problem-solving language of modern corporations is still coded in the speech of the more psychoanalytically oriented professions. Of course, not all these professions employ the language of the unconscious. Some professions will, therefore, be better able than others to help individuals to express their guilt or to understand why they are sacrificing their lives to a compound of desire and duty.

Certainly, it has been the work of the church in many generations to assist in the sacrificial transmutation of desire into duty. Indeed, the churches have promised to induct individuals into a kind of service that is more like perfect freedom, as if performing the duty of the disciple will fulfill the most basic and intense human desires. Even the transformation of desire into this sort of liberating duty, however, calls for new self-restraint to accompany the new sense of mission. In many cases this self-restraint amounts to a sacrifice of the spirit, a broken and contrite heart, perhaps. Failing that transformation, a more terrible sacrifice is in store for the individual who aspires to new status and satisfactions. That warning is indeed part of the meaning of the Daedalus complex.

When the church's services, primarily its rituals, work very well, they can indeed cut the emotional bonds that make duties heavy and perpetuate unnecessarily sacrificial lives. In fact, the churches' rites of initiation, baptism and confirmation, are intended to cut the ties of the individual to the family of origin in order to free him or her for more general and abstract obligations and to introduce him or her to a new kind of freedom. When youth is protracted well into the individual's twenties and even thirties, however, the emotional bonds of childhood are not so easily broken or even transformed.

Without sharp and ritualized breaks between the past and the present, the individual may engage in a process of maturing that allows early residues to operate beneath the surface of consciousness well into adulthood. In fact, Levinson (1978) notes that many men in their forties and fifties are still working on expelling these "ghosts" of childhood and in sorting out what dreams are worth keeping as sources of hope and motivation in their latter years. Under these conditions, individuals can easily be open to the churches' suggestions that they turn these underlying desires into new duties, rather than forge the instruments of their own liberation.

I am questioning the church's role in perpetuating emotional indebtedness, in turning desire into unnecessarily heavy duty, and in encouraging the individual to perform unnecessary sacrifices. Many of these sacrifices, like the unnecessary operations performed by the medical profession, have helped to sustain the church's own rather expensive organization. To cure the church of the Daedalus complex will mean that the church will have to draw on another set of motivations entirely, rather than profit from the recycling of emotional debt from one generation, or one stage in a person's life, to the next.

In this chapter I am also suggesting that the laity, far from being unconcerned over various social problems and issues, may be unable to accept the churches' leadership and exhortations to various forms of social engagement. Some of the laity may be rebelling at what may seem to them to be the exploitation of their ordinary human compassion by the church for its own agendas and programs. On the other hand, many of the clergy may feel so burdened by a sense of their own obligations and sacrifices that they are asking the laity to share their pastoral and social duties with them. I wonder whether many of the laity are aggrieved because they, like the clergy, have sought in the church relief from their own emotional and spiritual indebtedness, only to find that the church is asking them to shoulder heavier duties. Does the church ask its people to mortgage their lives as principal in an essentially unpayable debt owed to God for their salvation? What does the church actually do to enable the laity to resolve—rather than merely to recycle—their unpaid debt to their own desires and duties?

It is in the churches' interests to direct the individual's self-sacrifice, whether toward its own service or toward service to the world. Thus in exhortations to a life of such service, the churches may indeed be exploiting—but not resolving or satisfying—the residues of emotional debt that have not been paid off, either to primitive greed and anger, to the self, or to previous generations. Of course, the church may seek to provide solutions for the problems caused by its remedies, for example, relief through confessions of unworthiness and through pastoral care. But to give the illusion of solving self-generated problems is precisely the work of any emotional or social complex. That is what a complex does.

The churches' contribution to the recycling (rather than to the resolution) of emotional debt is no doubt somewhat more complex than I have been suggesting. By creating, like Daedalus, a set of votive offerings by which people can seek to restore their relation to nature and society, the church reinforces the desire for an unbroken relationship to the natural and social world. That relationship, I have argued, existed in the womb, and the memory of it—as well as the hankering for it—remains in the unconscious to create a heart that is indeed restless. The heart may not find its rest in the churches, however, precisely because the churches stimulate these unsatisfiable desires, turn them into additional and quite heavy duties, and perpetuate the call for the sacrifice of the heart, the soul, and the mind.

This continued mortgage on the self has two additional consequences that impede the churches' mission. On the one hand, it may intensify the laity's resentment at the sources of contradiction and uncertainty in their lives, that is, at the individuals and groups who threaten the laity's possession of their place in the community and in the succession of generations. Unpaid emotional debts to the self can also make it exceedingly difficult to hear with enthusiasm further clerical calls to selfless service either to the church or to the world.

The key to this complex, of course, is that the church creates the effects it deplores: the laity's conservative reactions to the sources of social disruption, the laity's longings for a peace that the churches promise and cannot give, and the churches' apparent inertia in the face of repeated exhortations to make the world a better place. This is not to ignore, of course, the many effective and valid social initiatives on the part of the church, whether at the grass roots or by denominational agencies. It is simply to say that the churches' complex feeds on itself.

To summarize: The churches perpetuate the unsatisfied longings and the burdens of unpaid emotional debts that they then seek to transmute, more or less effectively, into duty and sacrifice. The latter burdens, however, make the laity resentful of additional appeals to sacrificial action on behalf of the church and the world, a resentment that may be displaced onto those individuals and groups who make the community and nation a far cry from the heavenly city itself. The complex of problems lies within the church itself, therefore, rather than solely in the relation of clergy to laity, where it most dramatically comes to light.

The churches are not alone in this regard. Any community that seeks to restore primordial unities, to pay the debt of the individual to those who have gone before and to the world itself, is inevitably going to stimulate demands for an unbroken harmony with both the natural and social orders. That harmony will always be threatened by the young and the old, by aliens and intruders, and by those who represent impurities in the ideological or social system. No wonder, then, that communities claiming to be founded on such primordial harmonies will generate demands for purity. Someone must pay, even sacrificially, for the desires that have been thwarted or sublimated beyond recognition and beyond the hope for genuine satisfaction.

When it comes into play in complex societies, the desire for purity may reveal itself in hostility to foreign ideas and products, as is embodied, for instance, in the slogans "Buy American" and "Love America or leave it." No doubt such hostility is increasing under the impact of foreign investment in the United States. I would, therefore, expect that the United States will witness an increase in the number and intensity of attempts to purify American culture of alien elements, a new American Zionism. In its more concrete and specific forms, the desire for purity reveals itself in demands for the continued safety and enhancement of friends and neighbors, families and close associates at work or in play. These demands can be ethnocentric and racist, elitist and reactionary, but they stem from the same set of wishes for salvation that the churches themselves draw upon for membership and commitment.

Indeed, social movements often generalize this desire for purity beyond the protection of neighborhoods against invading ethnic outsiders to an environment free from pollution or to belief systems devoid of heresy.

Note how profound and plastic the underlying wish for access to the conditions of our origin really is. Even sociologists who deplore parochial religion and conservative attachments to concrete people and places argue passionately for an American society that is faithful to its traditions and founding symbols. But when social movements fail to take the desire for purity into the public arena through collective organization, individuals may seek that satisfaction for themselves either through the courts or through various forms of spirituality.

This demand for purity may therefore take the form of a search for judicial purgatives or spiritual cleansing, if the social order itself does not provide means of ridding social life of outside and contaminating influences. That demand will increase as each society becomes increasingly aware that its fate depends on the health or sickness, insanity or reasonableness, of individuals who live far beyond its borders. Disease and the products of hate cross international boundaries, as do capital, videos, music, and refugees.

Under these conditions it would be understandable if individuals once again turned to *daedaloi* who could promise them rescue, give them guidance through the labyrinthine paths toward achievement and recognition in their societies, or model for them an illusory transcendence. These new demands for purity may indeed inspire new calls for sacrifice. More dangerously for human freedom, the modern *daedaloi,* in the employment of the state as well as the church, may be called upon to offer a way out by protecting the nation from foreign influences, currencies, ideas, people, viruses, products.

Under these conditions it is especially important for both clergy and laity to identify the wish for purity as it appears in its many forms within the life of the congregation itself. Now, there is no direct way into the unconscious life of a community or a congregation, but there are indirect paths; one can search for indicators. Let me suggest one at this point. It is to ask who in one's congregation or community is being scapegoated. It may be the young, the poor, or the homeless, women, outsiders, or even the clergy.

Thus in any congregation there are several possible candidates for scapegoating. Certainly the young, who like Icarus "impede their fathers at their work" and seem to play when the serious rites of the community are at stake, can be scapegoated as a source not only of innovation but of threat to the community as a whole. In one congregation, however, the homeless were the object not only of concern but also of something approaching sheer dread. But there were reasons for this panic at the thought of incorporating the homeless into the life of the local congregation. That congregation was itself an ethnic group whose ties with the mother country had been seriously disrupted in World War II. Its members had been scapegoated during the war and were threatened with homelessness. Even their children had been abused on the streets and at school as enemy aliens. Aliens find it hard to welcome the homeless, who remind them of their own precarious hold on the fabric of social life.

In each case, one must ask oneself why the group in question is being scapegoated. Is it because they represent a threat to the continuity of the community or the congregation, as do outsiders and the young? Is it because they represent a source of disruption or of innovation, as do women and children who bring their own sources of inspiration and authority into the life of the church? Whatever disturbs the primordial social bonds of a community, based on affinity, family legacies, lines of descent, inherited ways of life, and cherished associations, can be seen as a threat to the womblike harmonies and to the continuity of the group in question. Until the church can help people with their own fears of spiritual homelessness, the conflicts between clergy and laity, liberals and conservatives, over social issues will remain on the surface, intractable and yet trivial in their grappling with the underlying issues of the heart and soul.

The Daedalus Complex
as Pastoral Hermeneutic

The Daedalus complex is most useful as a pastoral hermeneutic pointing to the most painful area where desires for purity and legacies of guilt come into play—in the relationships between the generations. When these are in tension, the pressures for sacrifice—or at the least for scapegoating—are likely to increase. That is because more is clearly at stake than the survival of a family, a congregation, or a way of life. In one sense the next generation represents an extension of ourselves: an embodiment of our own selves and not merely of what we represent and value. To be separated from that generation by a gulf, by an emotional or cultural divide, may therefore represent to many members of our congregations a fundamental flaw in their own lives. Separation, as Balint reminded us, can be experienced by some individuals as a basic fault within the self, precisely because it feels like the first separation from the sources of life. That is why Balint's patients underwent a period of mourning as they came to terms with that initial and perpetual separation from sources of life that had seemed to be permanent extensions of themselves. The clergy, too, may be needed to help one generation enable and, if need be, mourn the coming of age and passing on of another. Can the clergy enable that new generation to come of age and go on its way without coming to grief and without being burdened by unnecessarily heavy duty and sacrifice?

It may not be easy for the churches to interrupt the transmission of emotional indebtedness from one generation to the next; the churches' own rituals keep it alive without paying off and satisfying old debts or fulfilling old duties. Whenever rites of baptism or confirmation, of marriage or of burial, are performed, the unconscious uses them for its own purposes. While these rites are not always solemn, they are always serious, in the sense that powerful wishes are being aroused: wishes for primitive attachment and unity, desires for access to the sources of life, or even a hunger for the recognition of the voice that gives one life, even at the time of death. That is why so many communities, as I have noted, sing songs of lament even on such joyful occasions as a marriage, because the daughter is seen to be leaving home to become an alien and never to return.

If there is an element of seriousness on these occasions, we can be sure that the unconscious is listening and speaking from the depth of its own unsatisfied wishes and longings. Daedalus wept when he was preparing Icarus for the rites of initiation; he knew what sacrifices are inevitable when desire is transformed into duty and obligation. Despite themselves, then, the churches may be perpetuating unsatisfiable hopes for salvation and the sense of unpayable emotional debt, rather than enabling each individual, group, and generation to "let the dead bury the dead."

Nowhere is this issue more tangible than in the succession of the generations. Let us consider in more detail, then, one such instance: the relation of daughters to their mothers. The example chosen suggests that the Daedalus complex is not specific to men but is found across genders; it also suggests how difficult may be the task of enabling children to leave their spiritual homes and set out for themselves on their own spiritual journeys.

In *The Hungry Self* Chernin (1985) describes the "fateful encounter between a mother whose life has not been fulfilled and a daughter now presented with the opportunity for fulfillment" (1985:43). Chernin describes a situation in which the mother had dreams and longings that she could not fulfill; the daughter now bears the guilt of surpassing—and so symbolically rejecting—her mother's values and indeed her sacrifices. Like Icarus, the daughter rejects the instruction to stay within the parameters set for her, if only implicitly by the sacrifices her mother was willing to make. The conflict appears particularly in what Chernin describes as the "symbolic gender transformation" that women undergo while entering a predominately male occupational world (1985:52).

Clearly some women experience a "debilitating guilt" at the point in their lives at which they feel they are "surpassing the mother" (Chernin 1985:49). That guilt, of course, is intensified to the extent that the daughter unconsciously feels that she possesses magical powers over the mother and lives at her expense. This residue of infancy, in which the child seemed to be exhausting the mother and exerting magical controls over her, lives on in a feeling that the adult woman is responsible for her mother's emptiness and exhaustion. According to Chernin, by becoming bulemic or anorexic her patients act out their feeling of identification with mothers whom they see as fat or empty, drained or impoverished. In any event, these women end up needing to be fed and cared for themselves, either directly by their mothers or by a therapist. The longing for the mother, combined with residues of magical thinking, results in a terrible sacrifice of their own identities. They succeed, like Icarus, in destroying themselves, rather than in successfully leaving home. By manipulating food, they manage to share the fate of a mother who may never have left home and was herself confined to a constricted range of opportunities.

The fear of these women that they are living at the expense of their mothers is a fear that they wish to have. If that seems a bit harsh, simply remember that the fear is based on a desire to be fed in the most primordial of attachments: the attachment to the mother, which in the womb, and again at the breast, was quite literally at the expense of the mother. Over time, of course, the desire to drain the mother is sublimated into other desires, for example, for her attention, her other resources, and ultimately for her love and approval. This gradual transmutation of desire into duty is costly; someone must pay, and that someone is, of course, the self. In the end, Daedalus sacrifices to Apollo: a symbolic expression of the sacrifice that the myth already has described, in which Icarus pays dearly for his flight above and beyond the parameters set by his father Daedalus. No wonder, then, that Christianity offered a perfect sacrifice to end all sacrifices: a Son whose death pays the bill for all the transmutations of desire into duty.

The question I would ask is how each congregation ignores, arouses, exploits, or helps to alleviate and resolve these fears that Chernin and others have been treating in their own practices. These are the fears that one must pay for having lived at the expense of those who have given one life but whom one has nevertheless left and transcended by one's own achievements. The same fears create powerful resistance to the emergence of the true self. Unwittingly, the churches may collude with these resistances by reinforcing the feeling of individuals that they indeed have an emotional debt to pay or by presenting individuals with the opportunity to pay these debts through serving the organization of the church itself.

I should add, going back to Chernin's study of women with eating disorders, that women whose own opportunities had opened up included women whose mothers had had careers. Indeed, the fact that many of their mothers had enjoyed careers suggests that it was their mothers' fantasies rather than their real circumstances with which their daughters were identifying. That suggests, in turn, that the level of identification between daughters and mothers is at the level of the unconscious, where spiritual guidance and pastoral care must learn to tread if the church does not wish to intensify and exploit these women's longings for transcendence. Otherwise the church may unwittingly exploit their willingness to sacrifice, from one generation to the next. Indeed, one way to exploit that willingness is to turn the desire for true selfhood into a spurious form of spirituality, heavy on duty and the sublimation of desire, whether that duty is expressed in attending the altar or raising money for missions, that is, in what theologians have called "works."

Even the current enthusiasm for spirituality in the churches and the seminary may be due to the churches' unwitting perpetuation of the Daedalus complex. Wherever the church takes on itself the task of turning desire into duty, it will create a sense of unsatisfiable emotional debt. Whenever the church then tries to satisfy that debt by enabling the laity to make a wide range of relatively small sacrifices of time, talent, or whatever, the payments are inevitably costly and yet insufficient and need to be repeated from one generation to the next.

In fact, if the emphasis on spirituality does derive from heavy emotional duties, some of them perpetuated by the churches, there will be increased interest in the aspect of the Christian faith that cancels debts. That may take the form of a revival of interest in medieval formulas for the atonement or of biblical forms of the cancellation of debt, such as the jubilee year. The point is that the churches can diagnose what ails them partly by listening to the demands of the laity for specific forms of teaching and pastoral leadership.

At the risk of seeming unduly pessimistic, however, I want to observe that courses on spirituality, like movements of the spirit, may not be enough to produce a genuine form of relief or liberation of the individual from the burden of emotional debt. This cautionary remark is intended primarily for congregations in which Pentecostal spirituality is increasing. Even in Latin America, where the Pentecostal movement is liberating people from traditional obligations and constraints for a relatively new life of achievement, mobility, and political participation, the constraints on the spirit enter in almost from the outset.

The sociologist who has most clearly described this process is David Martin, in his recent book on the Pentecostal movements in Central and Latin America (Martin 1990). No sooner does the Pentecostal movement stimulate desires and raise expectations for a new and more abundant life than it also schools the believer into a set of new duties and obligations to work and to family. These entail the limitation of consumption and the postponement of many satisfactions; alcohol is especially prohibited, as is the excessive consumption of any food and drink. The believer begins to save money and limit leisure time to activities that do not interfere with work and self-improvement. Charisma, as Weber reminds us, brings with it new duties and imposes new forms of self-restraint even while appearing to liberate the individual from traditional ties to family or clan and from the ordinary or routine tasks of getting and spending.

The spirit often moves to stimulate a new asceticism: not only self-discipline and restrained consumption but also a commitment to realize the self over time. What appears to be self-realization in the present, then, becomes a promise of greater self-actualization in the future. More to the point, the emergence and recognition of the true self is subjected to a process of continual development. Self-discovery, then, becomes a process in which the true self does not fully arrive until it is disclosed at the end of time. Such a parsimonious expres-

sion of self-discovery may feed the laity's spiritual
hunger and underlie the feeling of many laity that they
have been shortchanged.

To mediate the generational passage without adding to
the complex of unsatisfied longings, unpaid debts, and
unnecessary sacrifices is an exceptionally difficult pastoral task, because unconscious meanings are so often
disguised in what appears to be ordinary language. Even
the specialized language of the liturgy, once a vehicle
for expressing many such meanings that elude everyday
speech, has been altered to conform more to ordinary
usage and has lost much of its resonance with the unconscious. Without training in the language of the unconscious, then, many clergy will be less well equipped
than some of their secular competitors to express and
relieve the suffering that accompanies the transformation of desire into duty.

I can think of no higher priority to be placed before
theological education and the continued education of
the ministry than training in the language of the unconscious. Failing to receive that training in turn from the
clergy, the laity will seek and find it elsewhere. This
"forgotten language," as Fromm called it, is still the language that can enable individuals and groups to lay
down the burden of debt and live with compassion
rather than sacrifice. Without access to the language of
the unconscious, those who seek to settle the account
between desire and debt and to offer sacrifice for the
debt owed to both nature and society will inevitably create a sacrificial system in which sources of disruption
and change will have to be eliminated.

Unless they master the language of the unconscious,
the churches will be unable to break the cycle of debt
and sacrifice from one generation to the next. Instead,
the church will continue to ignore, foster, or even create expectations of a world in which the perfect sacrifice
can be rendered and there will be no residues of guilt or

desire left over to be satisfied. These residues are the "offscourings," you may remember, the leftover votive offerings that were not wholly consumed by the sacrificial fires. They are reminders of the incompleteness of all attempts to restore blighted lives or to make up for premature deaths, a sign of the futility of magical attempts to undo what has been done or to "make up for lost opportunities."

There are always leftovers, aspects of unfinished emotional business, to remind the laity, and the clergy, that their rites are not wholly vivifying and their debts, therefore, not wholly satisfied. The clergy can own up to the fact that the churches' rites are no longer guarantees of the safe succession of the generations; the clergy themselves then can no longer be expected to take the responsibility and the blame for mediating that fateful transition. Unless the clergy and laity recognize that they are really equally vulnerable to a broken connection between the generations, they will continue to engage in a process of mutual scapegoating. As long as the clergy's sense of responsibilities extends far beyond the clergy's authority, they will take the task of mediating generational succession—and other pastoral tasks—to heart and be perfect targets for scapegoating.

It is precisely the willingness to live without salvation, that is, without heaven on earth, that will put an end to the sacrificial cycle, cancel the recycling of debt from one generation to the next, and prevent the process of scapegoating. On the other hand, if in promises of salvation the church keeps alive latent desires for purity among both the clergy and the laity, the complex cycle of turning desire into debt, paid for by sacrifice and scapegoating, will continue to divide the church and separate it from the rest of humanity.

The Daedalus complex will survive as long as the illusion persists that purity—salvation—is possible. Indeed, the possibility of escape from the island of Minos with its labyrinth and fatal Minotaur is shattered by the death of Icarus. The truth buried in the myth is that the debt to greed, to all-consuming desire, must somehow be paid; it cannot be deferred or ignored but must be resolved. Otherwise there is no escape from unmitigated tragedy. Nonetheless, just as the *daedaloi* fashioned the means for escape from such a fate for generations of devotees who were willing to pay dearly for their votive offerings, the church has offered the appearance of such an escape, salvation, to each generation that has been willing to believe that the church offers a means for transcending the common fate that waits at the center of the labyrinth, death itself.

Now, however, the churches' symbolic products are not simple carved statues to be burned on the altar; they are more likely to be the complex position papers and well-thought-out theological statements of the churches' *daedaloi,* its intellectuals that serve on various commissions and staff its agencies. The labyrinth has become in the meantime even more complex. Just try to read the minutes of any denomination's general assembly or convention, let alone the plethora of official statements and reports submitted for the guidance of the faithful. The *daedaloi* are still at work, and they will remain a privileged class living at the expense of the larger society as long as there is a demand for their services. The market for their symbolic products is based on the laity's guilt: the residues of the transformation of desire into duty. These residues require a sacrifice of the self, the spirit. The fact of that sacrifice, however, perpetuates the infantile sense that there is something wanting or flawed in the individual's inner self.

In Barfield's (1979:36) most recent work, he argues that such guilt derives from self-estrangement, a separation from our own humanity. It is this alienation that leads us to accept an overweening sense of responsibility for the harm inflicted by past generations on each other. Remember that George Will also was protesting against that use of guilt to promote a sense of social responsibility. This guilty form of social responsibility is far different, he argued, from a mature sense of responsibility for alleviating the suffering of others. What is called for, according to Barfield (1979:62), is a more realistic, and, I would add, compassionate reunion with humanity that comes from being in touch with our true selves. The church will therefore need to cast its lot with humanity without assuming that the faithful enjoy a hold on salvation not available to outsiders.

That "reunion with humanity" (to use Barfield's phrase) will require a fundamental change in the unwritten and often implicit or even unconscious expectations that the laity and the clergy have of each other. The willingness of clergy and laity to perform their celebrations outside the gates of Eden and in the mutual solidarity of a gladly acknowledged original sin may be the beginning of a new relationship within the churches. His yoke will be relatively easy and its burden comparatively light precisely because it will be no longer burdened with a desire for purity or the duty to sacrifice.

Bibliography

Anderson, Benedict. *Imagined Communities: Reflections on the Origin and the Spread of Nationalism*. London: Verso, 1983.

Baechler, Jean. *Suicides*. Translated by B. Cooper. New York: Basic Books, 1979.

Balint, Michael. *The Basic Fault: Therapeutic Aspects of Regression*. With preface by Enid Balint. New York: Brunner/ Mazel Publishers, 1979.

Barfield, Owen. *History and Guilt*. Middletown, Conn.: Wesleyan University Press, 1979.

Becker, Ernst. *Escape from Evil*. 2nd ed. New York: Free Press, 1976.

Bellah, Robert N., Richard Madden, William M. Sullivan, Ann Swidler, and Steven M. Tipton. *Habits of the Heart: Individualism and Commitment in American Life*. San Francisco: Harper & Row, 1985.

Berryman, Philip. "El Salvador: From Evangelization to Insurrection." In *Religion and Political Conflict in Latin America,* edited by Daniel Levine, pp. 58–78. Chapel Hill, N.C.: University of North Carolina Press, 1986.

Binion, Rudolph. *After Christianity: Christian Survival in Post-Christian Culture*. Durango, Colo.: Logbridge-Rhodes, 1986.

Bion, W. R. "Group Dynamics: A Review." In *New Directions in Psychoanalysis,* edited by Melanie Klein, Paula Heimann, and R. E. Money-Kyrle, pp. 440–77. New York: Basic Books, 1957.

Bracewell-Milnes, Barry. *Tax Avoidance and Evasion: The Individual and Society*. London: Panopticon Press, 1979.

Bulfinch, Thomas. *Bulfinch's Mythology*. The Modern Library. New York: Random House, n.d.

Burkert, Walter. *Ancient Mystery Cults.* Cambridge, Mass.: Harvard University Press, 1987.

————. *Greek Religion: Archaic & Classical.* Translated by John Raffan. Oxford: Basil Blackwell Publisher, 1985.

————. *Structure and History in Greek Mythology and Ritual.* Berkeley, Calif.: University of California Press, 1979.

Campbell, Angus. *The Sense of Well-Being in America: Recent Patterns and Trends.* New York: McGraw-Hill Book Co., 1981.

Campbell, Joseph. *The Hero with a Thousand Faces.* 1949 Bollingen Series, no. 17. Princeton, N.J.: Princeton University Press, 1972.

Cantril, Albert Hadley. *The Pattern of Human Concerns.* New Brunswick, N.J.: Rutgers University Press, 1965.

Capps, Donald. *Deadly Sins and Saving Virtues.* Philadelphia: Fortress Press, 1987.

Carroll, John. *Guilt: The Grey Eminence Behind Character, History, and Culture.* London: Routledge & Kegan Paul, 1985.

Charlesworth, James H. *Jesus Within Judaism: New Light from Exciting Archaeological Discoveries.* New York: Doubleday, 1987.

————, ed. *The Old Testament Pseudepigrapha.* Vols. 1 and 2. Garden City, N.Y.: Doubleday & Co., 1983.

————, ed. *The Old Testament Pseudepigrapha and the New Testament. Prolegomena for the Study of Christian Origins.* Cambridge: Cambridge University Press, 1985.

Chernin, Kim. *The Hungry Self: Women, Eating, and Identity.* New York: Harper & Row, 1985.

Coleman, James S. *The Asymmetric Society.* Syracuse, N.Y.: Syracuse University Press, 1982.

Cuddihy, John Murray. *No Offense: Civil Religion and Protestant Taste.* New York: Seabury Press, 1978.

————. *The Ordeal of Civility: Freud, Marx, Levi-Strauss, and the Jewish Struggle with Modernity.* Boston: Beacon Press, 1987.

Danforth, Loring H. *The Death Rituals of Rural Greece.* Princeton, N.J.: Princeton University Press, 1982.

Drabek, Thomas E. *Human System Responses to Disaster: An*

Inventory of Sociological Findings. New York: Springer-Verlag, 1986.

Eisenstadt, S. N. *Modernization, Protest, and Change.* Englewood Cliffs, N.J.: Prentice-Hall, 1966.

Erikson, Kai. *Everything in Its Path.* New York: Simon & Schuster, 1976.

Fox, Robin Lane. *Pagans and Christians.* San Francisco: Harper & Row, 1986.

Freud, Sigmund. *Character and Culture.* New York: Collier Books, 1963.

————. *Delusion and Dream, and Other Essays.* Edited by P. Rieff. Boston: Beacon Press, 1956.

————. *Group Psychology & the Analysis of the Ego.* 1959, with translation and editing by James Strachey. Reprint. New York: W. W. Norton & Co., 1975.

Girard, René. *Job: The Victim of His People.* Translated by Y. Freccero. Stanford, Calif.: Stanford University Press, 1987.

Gluckman, Max. *Politics, Law, and Ritual in Tribal Society.* 1965. Reprint. Oxford: Basil Blackwell Publisher, 1982.

Gutierrez, Gustavo. *A Theology of Liberation.* Maryknoll, N.Y.: Orbis Books, 1973.

Hodder, Ian. *The Present Past: An Introduction to Anthropology for Archaeology.* New York: Pica Press, 1982.

————. *Reading the Past: Current Approaches to Interpretation in Archaeology.* Cambridge: Cambridge University Press, 1986.

Huntingdon, Richard, and Peter Metcalf. *Celebrations of Death: The Anthropology of Mortuary Ritual.* Cambridge: Cambridge University Press, 1979.

Jaques, Eliott. "Social Systems as a Defense Against Persecutory and Depressive Anxiety." In *New Directions in Psychoanalysis,* edited by Melanie Klein, Paula Heimann, and R. E. Money-Kyrle, pp. 478–98. New York: Basic Books, 1957.

Josephus. *The Works of Josephus. B. J.* Book 3, chapter 10. Translated by William Whiston. Peabody, Mass.: Hendrickson Publishers, 1987.

Kaselman, Thomas A. "Ambivalence and Assumption in the Concept of Popular Religion." In *Religion and Political Conflict in Latin America,* edited by Daniel Levine, pp.

24–41. Chapel Hill, N.C.: University of North Carolina Press, 1986.

Klein, Melanie. "On Identification." In *New Directions in Psychoanalysis,* edited by Melanie Klein, Paula Heimann, and R. E. Money-Kyrle, pp. 309–45. New York: Basic Books, 1957a.

————. *Love, Guilt, and Reparation.* New York: Delacorte Press, 1975.

————. "Notes on Some Schizoid Mechanisms." *International Journal of Psycho-Analysis* 27 (1946): pp. 99–110.

————. "The Psychoanalytic Play Technique." In *Psychoanalysis,* edited by Melanie Klein, pp. 3–22. New York: Basic Books, 1957b.

Lane, Christel. *The Rites of Rulers: The Soviet Case.* Cambridge: Cambridge University Press, 1981.

Lasch, Christopher. *The Culture of Narcissism.* New York: W. W. Norton & Co., 1978.

Levine, Daniel, ed. *Religion and Political Conflict in Latin America.* Chapel Hill, N.C.: University of North Carolina Press, 1986.

Levinson, Daniel. *The Seasons of a Man's Life.* N.Y.: Harper & Row, 1978.

Lifton, Robert J. *The Broken Connection: On Death and the Continuity of Life.* New York: Simon & Schuster, 1979.

————. *Home from the War.* New York: Simon & Schuster, 1973.

Luhmann, Niklas. *The Differentiation of Society.* New York: Columbia University Press, 1982.

————. *Religious Dogmatics and the Evolution of Societies.* Translated by P. Beyer. New York: E. Mellen Press, 1984.

McGregor, J. F. "The Baptists: Fount of All Heresy." In *Radical Religion in the English Revolution,* edited by J. F. McGregor and B. Reay. 1984. Reprint. Oxford: Oxford University Press, 1986, pp. 23–64.

Manning, Brian. "The Levellers and Religion." In *Radical Religion in the English Revolution,* edited by J. F. McGregor and B. Reay. 1984. Reprint. Oxford: Oxford University Press, 1986, pp. 65–90.

Martin, David. *The Dilemma of Contemporary Religion.* New York: St. Martin's Press, 1981.

————. *Tongues of Fire: The Explosion of Protestantism in Latin America*. Oxford: Basil Blackwell Publisher, 1990.

Mendels, Doron. *The Land of Israel as a Political Concept in Hasmonean Literature: Recourse to History in Second Century Claims to the Holy Land*. Tübingen: J. C. B. Mohr (Paul Siebeck), 1987.

Mills, C. W. *Sociology and Pragmatism*. New York: Oxford University Press, 1966.

Mitchell, B. R. *Abstract of British Historical Statistics*. With Phyllis Deane. Cambridge: Cambridge University Press, 1962.

Moore, R. Laurence. *Religious Outsiders and the Making of Americans*. New York: Oxford University Press, 1986.

Neusner, Jacob. *Self-Fulfilling Prophecy: Exile and Return in the History of Judaism*. Boston: Beacon Press, 1987.

Niebuhr, Reinhold. *The Nature and Destiny of Man: A Christian Interpretation*. Vols. 1 and 2. New York: Charles Scribner's Sons, 1941.

Oakman, Douglas E. *Jesus and the Economic Questions of His Day*. Vol. 8 of *Studies in the Bible and Early Christianity*. Lewiston, N.Y.: Edwin Mellen Press, 1986.

Ovid. *Metamorphoses*. Translated by Rolfe Humphries. Bloomington, Ind.: Indiana University Press, 1955.

Parkin, David, ed. *The Anthropology of Evil*. Oxford: Basil Blackwell Publisher, 1985.

Pawlikowski, John T. "Jewish Approaches to Pluralism: Reflections of a Sympathetic Observer." In *Cities of Gods: Faith, Politics, and Pluralism in Judaism, Christianity, and Islam,* edited by Nigel Biggar, Jamie S. Scott, and William Schweiker, pp. 55–72. Contributions to the Study of Religion, no. 16. New York: Greenwood Press, 1986.

Rahman, Falzur. "Islam and Political Action: Politics in the Service of Religion." In *Cities of Gods: Faith, Politics, and Pluralism in Judaism, Christianity, and Islam,* edited by Nigel Biggar, Jamie S. Scott, and William Schweiker, pp. 153–166. Contributions to the Study of Religion, no. 16. New York: Greenwood Press, 1986.

Rank, Otto. *The Double: A Psychoanalytic Study*. Chapel Hill, N.C.: University of North Carolina Press, 1971.

————. *The Psychology of the Soul*. Philadelphia: University of Pennsylvania Press, 1950.

————. *Truth and Reality: A Life History of the Human Will.*
New York: Alfred A. Knopf, 1936.

Reik, Theodor. *Masochism in Modern Man.* 1941. Translated
by Margaret H. Beigel and Gertund M. Kurth. Reprint. New
York: Grove Press, 1957.

————. *Myth and Guilt: The Crime and Punishment of Man-
kind.* 1957. Reprint. New York: Grosset & Dunlap, Universal Library Edition, 1970.

Robbins, Thomas, and Roland Robertson, eds. *Church-State
Relations: Tensions and Transitions.* New Brunswick, N.J.:
Transaction Books, 1987.

Seldon, Arthur. "Prologue." In *Tax Avoidance: The Economic, Legal, and Moral Interrelationships Between
Avoidance and Evasion.* London: The Institute of Economic Affairs, 1979.

Shanks, Michael, and Christopher Tilley. *Social Theory and
Archaeology.* Albuquerque, N. Mex.: University of New
Mexico Press, 1988.

Shils, Edward. *Center and Periphery: Essays in Macrosoci-
ology.* Chicago: University of Chicago Press, 1975.

Smith, Brian H. "Chile: Deepening the Allegiance of Working-
Class Sectors of the Church in the 1970's." In *Religion and
Political Conflict in Latin America,* edited by Daniel Le-
vine, pp. 156–86. Chapel Hill, N.C.: University of North
Carolina Press, 1986.

Stambaugh, John E., and David L. Balch. *The New Testament
in Its Social Environment.* Library of Early Christianity, edited by Wayne Meeks. Philadelphia: Westminster Press,
1986.

Turner, Victor. *Dramas, Fields, and Metaphors: Symbolic
Action in Human Society.* Ithaca, N.Y.: Cornell University
Press, 1974.

————. *Process, Performance, and Pilgrimage: A Study in
Comparative Symbology.* New Delhi: Concept, 1979.

————. *The Ritual Process.* Chicago: Aldine Publishing Co.,
1969.

U.S. Congress. House Subcommittee on Oversight of the Com-
mittee of Ways and Means. *Underground Economy.* 96th
Cong., 1st sess., 1979. Serial 96-70.

Veyne, Paul. *From Pagan Rome to Byzantium.* Vol. 1 of *A*

History of Private Life. Edited by Philippe Aries and George Duby. Cambridge, Mass.: Harvard University Press, Belknap Press, 1987.

Wallace, Anthony. *St. Clair: A Nineteenth-Century Coal Town's Experience with a Disaster-Prone Industry.* Ithaca, N.Y.: Cornell University Press, 1981.

Wallerstein, Robert S. *Forty-Two Lives in Treatment: A Study of Psychoanalysis and Psychotherapy.* New York: Guilford Press, 1986.

Watts, William, and Lloyd A. Free. *State of the Nation III.* Lexington, Mass.: D. C. Heath & Co., Lexington Books, 1978.

Weber, Max. *On Charisma and Institution Building.* Edited by S. N. Eisenstadt. Chicago: University of Chicago Press, 1968.

Wilson, Bryan. *Magic and the Millennium.* London: Heinemann Education Books, 1973.

————. *Religion in Sociological Perspective.* Oxford: Oxford University Press, 1982.

Wilson, John F. *Public Religion in American Culture.* Philadelphia: Temple University Press, 1979.

Winnicott, D. W. *Home Is Where We Start From.* New York: W. W. Norton & Co., 1986.

Wuthnow, Robert. "The Growth of Religious Reform Movements." *The Annals of the American Academy of Political and Social Science.* 480 (July 1985): 106–116.

Zerubavel, Eviatar. *The Seven Day Circle: The History and Meaning of the Week.* Chicago: University of Chicago Press, 1985.

Index

abstract terms, 83–84
Adam and Eve myth, 52
aggression, 145
Anderson, Benedict, 19
androgyny, 44–45
anger, 19–21
Anglican *Book of Common Prayer*, 35, 60, 84
anxiety, 110–115
Arendt, Hannah, 92
asceticism, 187–188
Augustine, 143–144
Australian aborigines, 45

Balint, Michael, 109, 121–125, 145, 146, 147, 182
Barfield, Owen, 190–191
basic flaw. *See* fundamental fault; original sin
Becker, Ernst, 99
Binion, Rudolph, 132
Bion, W. R., 115
Book of Common Prayer. *See* Anglican *Book of Common Prayer*
Bracewell-Milnes, Barry, 161
Brawley, Tawana, 113
Bulfinch, Thomas, 14
bureaucracies, 66
Burkert, Walter, 14–15, 17, 27, 46–50, 82, 86, 89, 135–138

Campbell, Joseph, 34–35, 36, 40–41, 43, 44–45
Cantril, Albert Hadley, 164
Carroll, John, 102
Central America, 73
charisma, 71–73. *See also* original matrix; source of life
Chernin, Kim, 183–185
children, 150–151. *See also* infancy
Christianity, 31, 166–167. *See also* churches
churches: initiation ritual in, 175–176, 182; perpetuation of debt and, 28–30, 154, 165–167, 173–179; reunion with humanity and, 191; sin as social product and, 62–64
civic obligation, 27–28. *See also* modern societies
civic ritual, 13–14
"civil religion" hypothesis, 105
clergy, and conflict with laity, 173–174, 177, 179
Coleman, John, 155–157, 166
compassion, 173–175, 176–177, 191
compromise, 110–115
conservative political climate, 174–175